MW01259919

NOT JUST

ROOMMATES

YOUR ROADMAP TO MARRIAGE INTIMACY

SEAN REED

Not Just Roommates
Copyright © 2015 by Sean Reed

Dedicated To Lanette, Brandon, Brianna, and Brittani.
I'm forever grateful for you. It's my honor to serve you for the rest
of my life.

To my Family & Crossroads Church.
Your support and prayers throughout the years have been
life-changing.
Thank you.

Contents

Chapter 1

Not Just Roommates

A Roommate is defined as a person occupying the same house as another. When thinking of the word roommate, it doesn't produce images of an intimate, lifelong partnership. But in today's society, many married couples are only roommates.

In the rat race of life, spouses often get distracted from one another due to the demands of the day. By the time couples have a little down time from their busy demands, there's little gas left in the tank for real intimacy. Soon their focus is on paying bills, fighting traffic, and house chores. They're resembling roommates rather than lovers.

Roommates aren't required to have intimacy or to build a life together. They don't need to have a common vision. A roommate can create a contract that can be broken. But married couples are in a covenant. Bound together as one for life. Finding your shared interests, establishing responsibilities, and having a vision are vital to your success.

Early on in my own marriage, our thermostat of irritation was rising to a point where we were emotionally spent. Due to bumping heads on almost every subject in life, the breaking point arrived. Truth be told, we wondered if it was a mistake to get married altogether.

My wife of 17 years is now my intimate life-builder, but it hasn't always been this way. Our marriage was rough. If you looked up the definition of roommates, you would see our mug shots right there. We were physically attracted to one another, but we clashed on every facet of life.

She and I disagreed on most of the serious matters. We were divided over how to manage finances. Even arguing over simple things like where to grab a bite to eat. We lived with constant tension, anger, and stress. At one point we both wanted a divorce because we didn't know how to plug up the holes in our sinking ship.

We became roommates, playing our roles of the routine tasks of running a household. Every day, we went through the motions of parenting, cooking, and cleaning. Still we longed for more; we didn't sign up for a roommate lifestyle. There was a deep longing for an intimate and fulfilling marriage.

There we were. Two God-fearing, Bible-reading and ministry-leading people on the edge of falling apart. Yet it was right there in our greatest moment of weakness that we prayed and asked God to help us. He met us right there, and it was his strength and wisdom that brought us out. I sincerely believe that the blueprints for a successful marriage are wrapped up in the words of God. That's where things changed for my wife and me, when we chose to be wrapped up in the wisdom of God's word.

Not Just Roommates is written to show you how we overcame roommate status. It's straight talk that shows how you can support an intimate, life-building partnership. What I mean by intimate life-builder is that you're friends and not enemies. A decision is made to become partners in facilitating the vision of your home. This book helps you get a shared vision for your marriage that you build together.

In a healthy marriage you make time to do life together. Support one another's dreams, and keep up a healthy sex life. Build wealth, and budget together without fighting. Parent your children without division on how to raise them. You laugh with one another and travel the world together.

This book is worthless if not applied. Its purpose is to put y‿ on a pathway of success. Every chapter has a principle that you can pick up and plan. Pick up on a point that stands out to you, and plan how you'll apply it in your life. One thing you'll learn throughout the course of this reading is that you can't control your spouse. So read this book and ask God to show you what points are for you to pick up and plan.

Now please understand that my wife and I have moments of tension to this day. There are still days when she and I disagree on the best route to carry things out. She still has her way of seeing life that's different from mine, and that's okay with me. Two eyes can see a wider scope than one. I welcome her perspective, and she respects mine. Since we remain opinionated individuals, we could fight one another as we used to do. But now we do things God's way and our differences don't destroy us. We've matured in marriage and we matter more than the matters.

This isn't a book of myths, but true marital transparency. I want your marriage to prosper. It's your time! I brought up our marriage to say that if we made it back from the brink of divorce, you can, too. If you're not facing tough times in your relationship then great. This book is a source of wisdom and instruction. It will strengthen your bond of intimacy and vision.

I hope that you hear what I suggest and apply the insight that you find applicable to your relationship. What's the point of getting advice that won't be implemented? Use our experiences for your continued success.

I see it this way . . . if I were traveling through the jungle, and the forest was so dense that I couldn't see my way through it, I'd find a guide that knows how to get me to the other side. Someone who's previously blazed a trail can be my guide. I'd gladly follow their lead.

This book gives a map through the jungles of marriage. My wife, Lanette, and I made it through because we had great mentors and sought the help of wise counselors. We pursued the help of God himself. We surrendered to their advice, and we're better because of it.

Do you want a marriage success instead of a dreadful mess? Then create a home where you wake up every day next to your best friend instead of wishing the relationship would just end. You can create a home full of grace, love, mercy, and forgiveness.

If you both will listen and apply the principles in this book you can say, we're not just roommates. We are intimate life-builders.

Chapter Summary

- A roommate is defined as a person occupying the same house as another

- Roommates aren't required to have intimacy or to build a life together. They don't need a common vision; they can create a contract that can be broken

- Marriage Success is achieved by creating a home where you wake up every day next to your best friend instead of wishing the relationship would just end. It is a home full of grace, mercy, and forgiveness

Becoming Intimate Life–Builders:

1. Coordinate a time to read through and apply the principles in this book together.

2. Fully engage and participate; your relationship will only benefit from it.

3. Commit to the process. Remember you're building an intimate life-building partnership with your mate.

For Reflection:

- What do you consider the state of your marriage to be? Is it successful, failing, etc.? Why do you feel that way?

- What can you do to create your dream home? One that's full of grace, love, mercy, and forgiveness? What do you feel limits you from doing this?

Chapter 2

The University of Us

When we think of the word university, we typically think of a college campus. The word university can be defined as an institution of higher learning. This is correct, but there's a deeper meaning within the etymology of the word. It is a community of masters and scholars; unity in diversity. Now people may wonder why in the world I'd start a book on marriage with this definition. I'll get right to it.

To achieve unity in marriage, we can grasp a similar idea that we discover within the etymology of the word university. There must be unity while learning our differences. You see, the greater the unity, the stronger the bond, and the harder to break.

Ecclesiastes 4:9–12 (NLT): 9 Two people are better off than one, for they can help each other succeed. 10 If one person falls, the other can reach out and help. But someone who falls alone is in real trouble. 11 Likewise, two people lying close together can keep each other warm. But how can one be warm alone? 12 A person standing alone can be attacked and defeated, but two can stand back-to-back and conquer. Three are even better, for a triple-braided cord is not easily broken.

This passage makes plain the strength of togetherness. We enter marriage to be with a person we believe we are compatible with in life. Someone who's similar to us. This is a great concept until we spend more time with them. We soon discover our differences and imperfections. This is where a divide in the home can take place. Contempt and bitterness may creep in because the person we consider our partner and friend isn't being so friendly. At least their actions don't show what we consider respectful or loving behavior.

Within our society, we tend to believe actions speak louder than words. We want to see proof of love and commitment towards us.

The University of Us

When we don't get faithfulness or follow-through on promises or commitments in relationships, we draw back. Sometimes we even fight back. Why? I think because we are hurt and disappointed. Many times when a spouse has spoken loud and clear about what they need, and the other spouse fails to satisfy those requests, they get deflated or angry. How do you react when you have unmet expectations?

But if you look at that Scripture above, two are better. More than likely, you're better with them than you are without them. They may get on your nerves right now in the essential areas. But you saw something great in them that drew you into this relationship. If you can get past the smoke from the explosions in the home, you can see their value.

Note the tone within the text above: if one falls, the other can reach out and help; two people keeping each other warm; two back-to-back can conquer. This is a picture of support and fighting together. They're not fighting with one another; but fighting alongside each other. Instead of kicking the other person when they fall, they reach out to help them up. This is a picture of unity within diversity. These people are working together against an attacker and against the cold. What if that was the picture of your marriage? Two people united as one.

But every two people are different. God uniquely created them with different appetites, ideas, and emotions. Men and women have obvious differences, and some not so obvious ways of being. The wiring in our brains isn't the same. Women and men aren't hardwired to respond to circumstances of life the same way. This is a fact; not including the differences from our upbringing and environment. Yet a husband and wife are one unit. Like a left half and right half of a brain fused together to think as one mind.

Where we go wrong in relationships is in the assumption that the other person in the relationship should just "know." There's an expectation that people should understand what we're saying, as if communication is "common sense." But I'd suggest for a moment that there's no common sense, because our senses originated from different cultures. How we handle money or learned to think about finance may differ. Our expectations of sex or how we envision romance may be different. The manner in which we show affection or handle conflicts can be diverse. So here's my suggestion: build the University of Us. Create an institution of higher learning of your spouse; a community of masters and scholars, unified in our diversity.

What if we stopped judging the other person's motives and intentions for a moment? What if we stopped assuming they're out to harm us? For a moment, imagine that what may tick you off doesn't even bother them. So it's not a personal attack against you when they don't take the trash out upon request. When she was exhausted from a hard day's work and wasn't in the mood, she wasn't trying to harm you.

For a moment, sit down in the University of Us. Study your spouse's heart, mind, and body. Prepare yourself to learn how they think. Gain their perspective, and make an effort to see things from one another's side. If you open up and communicate in a non-hostile environment, you'll discover a person who's not out to hurt you. They love you, and aren't intentionally trying to harm you.

There's diversity within your marriage. Sometimes when we don't understand differences, we can become afraid or angry with the unknown. This is why marriage must be rooted in intimacy. It doesn't just work; it takes work. What kind of work, though? I believe class work. It puts us in a position to get to know them before assuming the worst. When couples fight against each other, they both end up hurt. When they work together, they can conquer any obstacle that comes against them. We're in this fight together.

Ecclesiastes 4:9–12 (NLT): 9 Two people are better off than one, for they can help each other succeed. 10 If one person falls, the other can reach out and help. But someone who falls alone is in real trouble. 11 Likewise, two people lying close together can keep each other warm. But how can one be warm alone? 12 A person standing alone can be attacked and defeated, but two can stand back-to-back and conquer. Three are even better, for a triple-braided cord is not easily broken.

You can help each other succeed as a unit. What if this mindset is applied to your family's future? When your spouse falls today, you could pick them up. If there was a negative prognosis from the doctor or a cold moment, your spouse can keep you warm. If we choose to stand alone when the attacks of life come we are susceptible to defeat. Choosing to walk in agreement enables you to conquer the complicated aspects of life. I'm persuaded that we can be deceived into believing that our spouse is our enemy. But let me ask you a question. What's the best way to destroy a home and get away with it? Get the homeowners to tear the home apart themselves. Listen to the words of Jesus:

Matthew 12:25 (HCSB): 25 Knowing their thoughts, He told them: "Every kingdom divided against itself is headed for destruction, and no city or house divided against itself will stand."

This brings us to our next chapter, where we'll discuss the real enemy. But I encourage you again: build the University of Us: an institution of higher learning of your spouse; a community of masters and scholars (us), unified in our diversity. Maybe this example will shed more light on the prize:

Imagine you're from America and I'm from Japan. Neither of us knows the other person's language or culture. You and I are placed on assignment together to manage a company that has operations in both the US and Japan. We are partners, and we need to work together to build this business. What can we change so that we can work together?

We've got to get to know one another. Both of us must learn each other's language and cultures to achieve success. There may be things that are normal in my world that are different from yours, from the food we eat to the way we worship.

Does this make you my enemy? Should I be angry with you because we are different? Everyone should answer, "no!" We should both have patience, willingness to learn, and a respect for one another. We are in this assignment together.

Well, at the University of Us, husbands and wives can learn of one another and merge their worldviews until they are united in the practical as they are in the spiritual realm through marriage.

Chapter Summary

- To achieve unity in marriage there must be unity while learning each other's differences

- Create a university within your marriage. Your "University of Us" where you both are the teacher and the student in order to learn of each other and achieve unity while learning your differences

- Everyone is different. God uniquely created you with different appetites, ideas and emotions. The wiring in your brains is not the same

- In the University of Us, study your spouse's heart, mind and body. Prepare yourself to learn how they think and gain their perspective

- Both of you must learn each other's language and cultures to achieve success

Becoming Intimate Life-Builders

1. Establish a University of Us for you and your spouse. You will both teach and learn of each other.

2. Ask your spouse about the things that they want out of life and your marriage. Be careful to respect their ideas and emotions

For Reflection:

- How well do you see from your spouse's perspective? How well do you truly know your spouse's heart and mind?

Resources

- The 5 Love Languages by Gary Chapman

Chapter 3

Inner Me or Enemy?

When there is no enemy within, the enemies outside cannot hurt you.

~Winston S. Churchill

We aren't in the fight for our marriage alone. Before discussing our adversary, we should first discuss our Advocate. Jesus, our Advocate, will never leave us nor forsake us. He's with us till the end. He's more powerful and glorious than our adversary. Jesus has authority and power over all the attacks against our marriage. The good news is that he's given that same power and authority over darkness to you.

John 10:10 (NLT): 10 The thief's purpose is to steal and kill and destroy. My purpose is to give them a rich and satisfying life.

The thief here is Satan. Let's face it; evil exists, but so does good. The kingdom of darkness is at war against the kingdom of light. God's children of light are constantly under attack from the kingdom of darkness. There are dark spiritual forces we cannot see. They're hard at work to steal, kill, and destroy families. But the good news is that Jesus has come to us to give us a rich and satisfying marriage.

Why is this relevant? Because you may think that your spouse is your biggest problem, but they're not. They are the one you can see and blame for your pain. But the mission statement of Satan is written in John 10:10. You know that your spouse isn't Satan. The sooner you realize that, the sooner you can fight the real enemy and win together.

God's picture of marriage is three joined in one. Check out these verses of Scripture:

Matthew 19:4–6 (NLT): 4 "Haven't you read the Scriptures?" Jesus replied. "They record that from the beginning 'God made them male and female.' 5And he said, "This explains why a man leaves his father and mother and is joined to his wife, and the two are united into one." 6 Since they are no longer two but one, let no one split apart what God has joined together."

Notice the male and female in the beginning with God. God made them and joined them as One. Last chapter we discussed that two are better than one and that's awesome, but check out the last verse of that passage we read earlier:

Ecclesiastes 4:12 (NLT): 12 A person standing alone can be attacked and defeated, but two can stand back-to-back and conquer. Three are even better, for a triple-braided cord is not easily broken.

Three are better: God + You + Your Spouse= better God + You + Your Spouse= Not easily broken!

What an equation! You aren't separate anymore. Sadly, there are married individuals with a single person's mentality. Living with separate bank accounts, secret social media relationships, and blocking out their spouse's access to their electronic devices. That's not unity. Your world has merged with your mate's. Upon declaring your vows before God you commit to Oneness. It's an agreement of dedicated openness and intimacy. Anything less is roommate status.

So if you were Satan, what strategy might you carry out to bring the house down? You must divide the oneness to conquer. Why?

Matthew 12:25 (HCSB): . . . Every kingdom divided against it-

self is headed for destruction, and no city or house divided against itself will stand.

The enemy will throw the rock and hide the hand. How does this work? Without exhaustively going into this topic, the general idea is the accusing of others. Satan's strategy is to recruit us to cast blame and place judgment on our spouse. His goal is to get you offended by your mate. They'd push a sensitive button to set you off.

That button may be the way harsh way that they spoke to you. It could be they're a workaholic and never make time for the family. Are they gentle towards the children, but short-tempered towards you? You may notice that the person is the life of the party with friends but is closed off around you. They may fail to execute on paying a bill you asked them to pay on time. I could go on for days, but the point is to get you offended, hurt, or angry. Because then you'll respond to them out of that pain, instead of God's word. It's been said time and again that "hurt people, hurt people."

This cycle must be broken, but how will we do this? Well, that's what this entire book is about. The first step is to realize whom you're fighting against. Your spouse may not know that you're as hurt or frustrated as you are. Remember, you're different!

Satan is behind the hurt. Your spouse is your friend. They may do things that offend you, but so did you towards God. Yet God still calls us sons and daughters. We are God's family despite our imperfections. His love covers our sins instead of exposing them and demanding justice. In order for us to move forward and get real progress in marriage, we must see the unseen. Discern the manipulative hand behind the rock thrown.

The reason this point is so crucial is that we expect our spouse to know us. The expectation is that they should automatically know what we expect. They are held to such a high standard of customer service that there's no way that they could measure up.

If they must earn your love through perfect customer service, then you can pack it up now and call it quits. It's an impossible standard.

They can't be perfect for you; that's God's place in the marriage. Your spouse isn't your Jesus. They can never be perfect. But because of Jesus within us, we can stay loving towards them. If we react in love towards our spouse before jumping to conclusions, we begin to silence the voice of accusations from our enemy.

Do you see what I see?

What if there is a bigger picture? What if your marriage was so important to the world that the kingdom of darkness takes notice of it and tries to destroy it? This is truth! So you should stop fighting your spouse and fight with your spouse. In the Book of Job we witness a conversation between Satan and God. There's not enough space in this book to get into every nugget, but for a little perspective's sake, let's examine a few verses:

Job 1:6–7 (NLT): 6 One day the members of the heavenly court came to present themselves before the Lord, and the Accuser, Satan, came with them. 7 "Where have you come from?" the Lord asked Satan. Satan answered the Lord, "I have been patrolling the earth, watching everything that's going on."

Do you see what I see? Satan is watching and then accusing. Satan is trying to provoke wrath and anger for crimes committed. So he goes through the earth watching the mistakes and sins of men. Keeping record of people's flaws and pitfalls. Critically pointing out our failures towards God's perfect laws so that we might be punished.

He brings these failures before God to get him to hold sinners accountable. He wants mankind to be separated or divided from their relationship with God. God, being a righteous Judge, can't allow our imperfections to go unpunished.

This is why we should offer thanks to Jesus, who bore the punishment for our sin on the cross! Our imperfections are covered in the blood of Jesus. Now our Heavenly Father sees us according to relationship rather than our performance. Love isn't earned, it's simply given! What would our marriages be like if our love was given regardless of the performance of our spouse?

Yet Satan is still at work in our homes, on our jobs, and in our cars. What's he doing? Bringing accusations that'll lead to condemnation and punishment. He wants you to feel as though your spouse doesn't love you, working meticulously to supply evidence of their lack of trustworthiness. Presenting proof to your mind that suggests that they're out to harm you. He uses their failures and shortcomings to justify why you should leave. Why you should withhold sex from them, or a giving you a good excuse to curse them out in a burst of anger. But he's a liar, and the truth isn't in Satan. This is why Paul wrote to the Church at Ephesus:

Ephesians 4:26–27 (NLT): 26 And "don't sin by letting anger control you. Don't let the sun go down while you are still angry, 27 for anger gives a foothold to the devil.

Don't give Satan another inch in your relationship. Walk in God's power of forgiveness and grace towards your spouse. As you learn of your differences, you'll discover that the majority of what appears malicious is a misunderstanding. Soon you'll grow to a place in your relationship where there's no war between one another because you recognize the real enemy.

One final thought on this enemy. Peter gives us a word of wisdom about our enemy's intent:

1 Peter 5:8–9 (NLT): 8 Stay alert! Watch out for your great enemy, the devil. He prowls around like a roaring lion, looking for someone to devour. 9 Stand firm against him, and be strong in your faith. Remember that your Christian brothers and sisters all over the world are going through the same kind of suffering you are.

You aren't the only one going through pain in marriage. Stay faithful in believing God. Stand firm against the devourer of marriages. Give no territory to your real enemy. He's like a roaring lion, searching for someone to take out.

Who is the person that's an easy prey for the predator? It's the person who refuses to walk soberly. Sobriety is clarity of thought, a mind untainted by deception and lies about their spouse. Any man or woman refusing to walk in grace and mercy towards others is a perfect target.

So be watchful and faith-filled, because Jesus has given us victory over our enemy. We've got to walk in that victory, and it starts with walking by faith. Live in alignment with God's word. We can't walk in bitterness and unforgiveness while expecting good success in marriage. We can't fight our spouse and expect to win with them.

You're not my enemy, you're inner-me ~ Sean Reed

Chapter Summary

- Jesus, our Advocate will never leave us nor forsake us. He is more powerful and glorious than our adversary

- God's picture of marriage is three joined in one.

- GOD+ you+ your spouse = better

- GOD+ you+ your spouse= Not easily broken

- Realize who you are really up against. Satan is behind the hurt.

- Satan brings accusations that lead to condemnation and punishment. He works meticulously to supply evidence of their lack of trustworthiness using their failures and shortcomings to justify why you should leave

- Walk in God's power of forgiveness and grace towards your spouse

Becoming Intimate Life-Builders

1. Establish oneness with your spouse by making the choice to fight for your marriage

2. Choose to forgive your spouse of the offenses that you're holding against them

3. Kick Satan and his accusations out of your ear and invite God to teach you how to love your spouse in spite of what may be many flaws

For Reflection:

- Take a few moments to ask the Holy Spirit what is true about your spouse. Write those things down and recite them so that they will be written on your heart concerning them.

Chapter 4

Two-Gether

Do two walk together unless they have agreed to do so?

~ Amos 3:3 (NIV)

Becoming intimate life-builders requires a powerful tool called agreement. I'm from St. Louis, Missouri. When we visit our family back home, there are several things that must be considered. Think about it. If you and I were trying to go to Missouri from Texas, we could travel several routes to get there. But that's assuming we're driving. Maybe we should travel via bike, or possibly by plane.

Depending on how we're getting where we're going, it changes the plans of the passengers drastically. The luggage changes, rental cars may need to be added, and how much it costs is adjusted.

A husband and wife may think that they're on the same page about their life plans. But in reality they're assuming that their spouse thinks the same way they do. Assumptions can lead to major dysfunction. Getting to Missouri from Texas is a big goal, with many pathways to get from A to B. There are so many preferences to be sorted out. Many details that need to be addressed and hopes expressed.

In most marriages the details of where, how, and when are shady. The danger with this ambiguity is that the ingredient of agreement gets lost in our silence or within the chaos of our conflicts. This is where real conflict and contempt can grow. Division within the vision creeps in within our assumptions. The assumption that our spouse gets our perspective, timetables, or strategies is faulty logic. We need to agree.

Fights over money, parenting strategies, religion, and sexual preferences (or the lack of sex at all) are leading causes for divorce. People are fighting, but why? Well, I believe that we take our disagreements personally. People even consider irreconcilable differences as grounds for divorce. It's possible that some people stay in the marriage but give up on God's best because they lack a shared vision.

Walk Together

Have you ever taken it personally when a waitress got your order wrong? "I said no onions!" Don't you hate it when people aren't hearing what you said with clarity while they looked you right in the eyeballs? "What do we have to do to get great service around here?"

Honestly, dissatisfaction with your spouse's service isn't grounds for divorce. It's grounds for a plan of agreement. Differences aren't always grounds for divorce. If there's sin in a relationship, such as adultery or abuse, then there are grounds for divorce. But sometimes the two just can't see together. Scripture asks a proper question: do two walk together unless they agreed to do so?

That's what takes place within the marriage covenant: two agreed to be one. In every area of life you both must be agreed on a plan of action. Obviously there will be negotiations here since you each differ in preference and culture. Within a marriage covenant, our souls are interconnected. There's a bond, a unity in a spiritual realm that's been merged by God himself. Our worlds, with all of their uniqueness, made a collision.

When cultures collide it can get ugly. If one of you prefer the house to be perpetually cleaned and the other says, "I'll get around to it," there will be conflict. There's no sin there, no grounds for divorce . . . just a clash of cultures. Your upbringing may have defined a dirty house as a sin. Your spouse may have grown up with a mentality of home being a place of relaxation and views cleaning as work. This is a clash of cultures, and a plan is needed to help you see together.

In a case like this, if you attend the University of Us, where you are both students and teachers, you could get traction. If a couple leaves the anger out of the classroom; if they refuse to insult their spouse with a critical tongue and instead hear one another out, they can find common ground. They can get creative and work towards solutions that'll make them both comfortable. Create cleaning systems for the house on one hand and off days for the other.

Since each marriage is different, I won't even try to put out every fire. But you get my point. A healthy marriage must come to agreement, or anger will simmer underneath the surface. Frustration and irritation will just keep churning within, and sooner or later, someone will explode or implode. Neither one of those options is God's best.

Remember, the enemy isn't your spouse. They're just different, and they don't get you. Don't nitpick at them and try to fix them because in all actuality, you may try to make them you. They are not, and never will be. They don't see everything like you, but that doesn't mean you must separate, just negotiate.

Ultimately, you're both trying to get to the same place: a fulfilled marriage. You may need to plan out how to get to your destination. What do you need for the journey to comfort you along the way? What compromises can you both make to see together?

The Power of Prayer

My encouragement to all couples reading this book is: pray! Pray for your spouse, not just about them. Lift them up before your Heavenly Father and ask for wisdom on how to love them.

Ask God for clarity of the vision for your marriage. Seek him for strength to overcome the inner battles that your marriage may face.

I hope you believe in the power of prayer. There's power released from heaven into your relationship. In conversations with The Counselor of your soul you can release problems beyond your control. Ask God to help you both to come into agreement on a plan for your home.

A word of caution: When you don't pray, whose power are you relying on to keep your home together? If you're depending on your own power, are you trying to control your spouse? Are you trying to fix them so you'll get the peace you want in your home? Please hear me; you can't control your spouse and get away with it. It'll always backfire on you. A person knows when they're being abnormally used or abused. I don't think that anyone reading this book is lining up to be manipulated. Why would we want to do this to the love of our life?

Instead, I urge you to take frustrations to God in prayer. Why would I place this particular point about prayer at this place in the book? Because there are moments when you want them to be on "your level" of commitment in the relationship. You may be ready to plan and get into agreement, but they may not be there yet. To force or coerce them to conform to your level of maturity is counterproductive. It may work temporarily, but it won't last.

You and your spouse need help from God. But divine intervention isn't the result of whining about why we are ticked off. God moves when we pray for people in love. He responds like a warrior aiming to win a battle when we pray in faith for our spouse.

Something happens within you when you pray for them as if they were yourself! It's hard to pray in love for a person you hate. It'll eat away at you until you realize there's something that needs to change within you. As a child of God, you shouldn't carry these negative emotions about a person. God will work on your heart while you're praying for theirs.

Prayer Brings Divine Intervention

Many people don't realize that God is in their marriage. Are you angry and fed up? Maybe it's because you're not prayed up. I cannot stress to you enough how prayer kept our marriage together. Seeking the Lord's help and sometimes just confiding what I was feeling gave me release. It's like a pressure cooker that was about to explode and prayer was my release valve. This way I didn't explode on my wife. You see, if my wife and I are one, then that means when she's hurting, I'm hurting. If you were sick, what would you want for your healing?

Ephesians 5:28–30 (NLT): 28 In the same way, husbands ought to love their wives as they love their own bodies. For a man who loves his wife actually shows love for himself. 29 No one hates his own body but feeds and cares for it, just as Christ cares for the church. 30 And we are members of his body.

This passage shows a powerful principle of nurture and care. No sane person would harm themselves, but instead takes care of their body when it's hungry and cleans it when it's dirty. You care for your needs. The same should apply to your mate. That, my friend, is true intimacy!

You are both one. In this passage it's directed towards the husband. Paul says a man shows love for himself by how he treats his wife. If I looked into your home, rode in your car with you or hung out with you, would I be able to see that you care for your spouse? I bet I could tell you cared for yourself. You'd eat, entertain, educate, and rest yourself. In the same manner that Christ is one with his Church and gave of himself for her, men ought to give of themselves for their wives.

See, in God's eyes, the two literally become one. You can be in separate buildings, but God sees you as one. That's why you share the name and wear the rings. So that others can see you are together. God doesn't need the rings or to see the name to acknowledge your union. We should try to get to the place where we see it just the same.

James 2:8 (NLT): 8 Yes indeed, it is good when you obey the royal law as found in the Scriptures: "Love your neighbor as yourself."

In what ways are you loving your spouse as yourself? In what physical actions are you communicating love to your spouse? Going to work to pay bills isn't a good answer because if you were single, you'd still have to work. Cleaning the house is good, but you'd do that if you were on your own. In what ways are you showing love to yourself, I mean your spouse? How do you nourish and care for your spouse? What open displays of affections, servitude, and friendship do you display?

This is why getting on the same page is important, because you need to know how to show them love in a manner they'll appreciate.

Example: I love cake, and my wife loves brownies. If I were to give her a special gift to communicate my appreciation, it's safe to say that brownies are the way to her heart. But selfishness or a lack of understanding may cause me to present a cake to her instead. Since I like cake, she should like it as well. So I'll give her what I want. She may gladly receive it, but I'm not completely meeting her need as much as my own.

To get on the same page, you must become servants of one another. My father and mother raised me with chivalry. I was taught to open doors and pull out a chair for a lady. My wife wanted me to treat her special, and this gesture is one way that I do that. Yet she'd open the doors first. It wasn't personal on her end, but it bothered me that I couldn't show her chivalry. So one day we talked about it. She didn't even notice she'd been blocking my hospitality. She now slows down at the door to give me the opportunity to treat her like a queen. Sometimes she forgets, but overall it works now since she and I are in agreement together.

Although these are small examples, I hope you both conclude that you must agree. It's an accumulation of many small issues that combine to appear to be a major issue! As we win the smaller battles we get traction. We gain experience, and when faced with a greater issue in marriage it'll be easier to get on the same page faster. In the next chapter we'll discuss something that'll help to take your relationship to the next level.

Chapter Summary

- Becoming intimate life-builders requires a powerful tool called agreement

- A husband and wife may think that they're on the same page about their life plans. In reality they're assuming their spouse thinks the same way they do. ASSUMPTIONS CAN LEAD TO MAJOR DISFUNCTION

- Pray for your spouse, not just about them. Lift them up before your Heavenly Father and ask for wisdom on how to love them.

- It's hard to pray in love for a person you hate. It'll eat away at you until you realize there's something that needs to change within you

- Without agreement, the accumulation of many small issues combine to appear as a major issue. Gain traction by agreeing on the smaller battles.

Becoming Intimate Life-Builders

1. Remove assumptions in your marriage by seeking agreement regarding every aspect of your lives. Discuss your preferences as exhaustively as needed

2. Make the decision and begin to pray for, not just about your spouse, remembering to pray in love.

3. Become a servant of one another and express to one another the ways that you attempt to serve.

For Reflection:

- What small issues have you allowed to accumulate into big problems in your relationship? This can also be identified by what is dysfunctional in your home

Chapter 5

Discovering Your Values

You never know how much you really believe anything until its truth or falsehood becomes a matter of life and death to you.

~ *C. S. Lewis*

Have you grown frustrated with unmet expectations? Your mate isn't meeting a need or fulfilling desires. There are ways of thinking that we all have. These ways of seeing life are almost sacred to us. One might define them as being foundational to our beliefs. Values become a part of who we are. In marriage, values mistakenly aren't clarified, and eventually there's a clash of cultures.

When you feel all warm and mushy because you two were thinking the same thing, this is an area of value agreement. When they strike a nerve of discord and there's dissension, there may be values and beliefs going to war. Statistically, the list you're about to read contains the top reasons for divorce in America. This isn't exhaustive, but it's a shortened snapshot of conflicts in values:

- Money fights are major: Most marriages that end in divorce call it quits over money fights. Is your spouse failing to meet a need here? Are you in agreement on a financial plan?

- Communication deprivation: Are you frustrated with the

over-abundance or lack of conversation? Tired of the manner in which they respond or don't respond to you?

- Let's talk about sex: Everyone has preferences and needs in this area. The last thing you want in a marriage is an unmet expectation in the bedroom. Sometimes infidelity has destroyed families.

- Parent with me please: Are you involved in correcting and connecting with your child? What's the plan for their educational development? Do you both see disciplining your child differently?

- Fights over faith: Couples are in disagreement from topics like which church to attend to what faith to believe. One person may want to be at church more often, the other may not want to go at all. They lack agreement in spirituality.

How do I define values?

Values are our tightly held beliefs and guiding principles of how we conduct ourselves. It's how we think the world should revolve around us. Our values are shaped by our upbringing, experiences, and lessons learned. Some of our values are good and some may not be. In marriage we may not share the same priorities or values. We are, by God's design, different. But differences aren't grounds for divorce.

If we will be successful at intimacy, we must grow from complaining about wants to negotiating our needs. If you get frustrated and withdraw from your mate when they fail to meet your needs, you'll never communicate effectively what you want. How can they ever meet an unspoken need?

Now you may say you told them before and you're tired of telling them because they won't change. But what if God took that kind of approach toward us? God is perfect, and deserving of our best. He's the greatest communicator! So he perfectly communicates with you, even though you still fail to get it right every time.

Regardless of your shortcomings, God's love and commitment for you is unconditional. Make it your goal to strive to be like Jesus, even in repeating your desires with your spouse. It's like everyone loves amazing grace until they have to give it to someone else.

It's time to stop the yelling and throwing tantrums to get what we want. There's no place for stonewalling a spouse to get results. It's unproductive; in fact, it's destructive! What is constructive is having two levelheaded people meeting in love to discuss their needs. Two self-controlled individuals who mutually and maturely plan ways to meet those needs. It's that simple.

I'm no mind reader

The assumption that a person "gets" what you want is false. You differ from one another, and must be informed most of the time what you need. Your spouse isn't a mind reader. They don't live their day with your every wish on their minds. It's a lofty expectation that'll always end in frustration.

Imagine going into a restaurant and desiring a menu item, but you never give your order to the waitress. You'd be hungry and angry because they didn't bring you what you wanted, but in reality it's a failure to communicate. Even worse, what if you came in and sat down, but there was no menu to choose from in the first place?

The waitress wouldn't even know what to serve, and you wouldn't know what to order. Neither of you can read minds, so you need insight to get it right. Couples need a menu, and they need to swap roles of servant and customer. At the University of Us you create menu items and tell them how you like it. They may not get it right off the bat, but you're a great teacher, and they're a great learner.

I often go to Cracker Barrel for breakfast. We order from the same waitress, with the same menu when we go. We are at a point now that before I open my mouth to order, she knows what I want. She's no mind reader! It's because I'm consistently going to the same waitress, asking for the same items. Now and then I'll switch it up and they're shocked at first, but then they make it happen. (I always give great tips, hint hint! Give them appreciation for a job well done. Even applaud them when they didn't do so well.)

Discover your values

Remember, your enemy isn't your spouse. They're different, and you can't expect them to be all-knowing of your values. Don't nitpick at them and try to fix them, because in all actuality you may try to make them you. Keep in mind, they don't see everything like you do, but that doesn't mean you need to separate, just negotiate.

I've created a values exercise you can download at www.not-justroommates.org. This will help to get the vision and values conversations rolling. Your goal here is to gain insight into the values of your spouse. Then from there, compare your top priorities and values to your spouse's results. Most times we've discovered that our preferences are different. That's okay!

The chart becomes a conversation piece to build a vision. To learn what your spouse prefers in the bedroom, finance, parenting, and so forth, this is a great place to start.

When my wife and I invested our time, money, and energy around our values, everything changed for the better! We needed this exercise before marriage. I encourage you to download this resource and build your life around your values.

As you discover your values, engage in effective communication instead of ineffective communication.

- Ineffective communication: yelling; throwing tantrums to get what you want; stonewalling your spouse; shutting them out; one-word answers; name-calling; throwing their past in their face.

- Effective communication: Two levelheaded people meet in love to discuss their needs and plan ways to meet those needs.

This is the foundation from which you build the University of Us. Your institution of higher learning of your spouse; a community of masters and scholars, unified in our diversity.

Your values are your core beliefs on how life should be lived. You'll defend these values because you believe that they are a part of who you are at your core. Without realizing it, couples may defend their values all the way to divorce court. Instead, I encourage you to develop values for your home that you can agree on.

The Power of Vision

The only thing worse than being blind is having sight but no vision.

~ Helen Keller

I have two eyes, yet I see one vision. If I were to close one eye, my sight becomes limited. It's not that I can't see, I just can't see the whole scope of vision, as I would with both eyes open. I have two different eyes and when I open them both, I see more than I did with one eye shut. But my sight isn't divided, because my eyes are united. This, my friends, is the power of a marriage vision.

You don't see a divided vision even though you use two separate eyes. The brain combines their individual input to form a singular image. This is simple, yet it's profound. You can have two individuals who see uniquely working a plan together. When a couple is united intimately, they can build infinitely. When you build the University of Us and discover your values, you can see a greater scope of vision when together. Both minds are like the eyes, joined to widen the life-building process.

Now, there are many books out there on vision. When most people think of marriage, they don't think about vision. But I believe that two must walk together in agreement. Develop a shared vision from finance to romance, parenting to vacationing. I'd like to go a step further and say, create a shared vision in every area of life.

Think about it; how will you discipline your children? One person may believe in spankings and the other person doesn't. That's a war waiting to happen. Another way to see the lack of a plan here is that it's an opportunity for dissension. One person may like to spend all the money that comes into an account before the money clears the bank, while their spouse is a super saver. A guy wants to live in the country, but she dreams of living downtown. She wants to do world missions, and he wants to build a medical practice in the inner city.

Our dreams, hopes, and desires are personal, so vision is powerful. Dreams and goals are attached to us and are precious. When we merge with one another in marriage, we bring all of our expectations and aspirations, our traditions and wishes. A vision gives clarity and keeps you both restrained from separating from the same path:

Proverbs 29:18 (NASB95): Where there is no vision, the people are unrestrained, But happy is he who keeps the law.

I think that it's possible to take two people who are polar opposites and they can work together at accomplishing great things. If they can learn to support each another and get the right mind-set about their differences, things will improve. Marriage is sometimes negotiation, but if God has merged you together, then you can do this with patience and persistence.

My wife and I plan everything together. We discuss everything from budgeting to grocery lists to vacations and child development.

The Power of Vision

This doesn't make us militant, and I don't feel like less of a man. She doesn't feel as if she's lost her identity. A vision helps us to get on the same page and walk together in moving our lives towards the place that God has called us to. The right questions help us to discover the right answers. Is your home perishing in an area? Well, Solomon gave us the key to revival in an area of decline. If there's no vision, we will struggle to succeed.

Now sometimes, it's not failing to plan, but it's a failure to follow through. God helped my wife and me with the lack of follow through. We were good talkers, and early in our marriage great at debate. Not so great with the follow through part though.

What changed? Desperation! We became sick and tired of seeing the same results of frustration and failure. There came a point where accountability to a drastic lifestyle change took place in our home. Over time we matured into being responsible, vision-oriented people. Our marriage and children are better because of our drastic maturation.

Set a time to talk with your spouse in a loving, respectful manner about moving forward in this area. I believe that you'll experience tremendous results. Later in a chapter titled Set It or Forget It, we'll talk about the use of technology for reminders.

I suggest that you find and connect with mentors that can hold you accountable to your vision. Tell them what you both want to achieve. Be honest with them about your progressions or regressions as you meet up with them throughout the year. These are the steps we took to grow beyond being talkers to walkers. Never will I revert to a life without shared vision. Thankfully, we're awakened to the power of vision.

Chapter Summary

- Values are our tightly held beliefs and guiding principles of how we conduct ourselves. Our values are shaped by our upbringing, experiences and lessons learned.

- If we will be successful at intimacy, we must grow from complaining about wants to negotiating our needs

- As you discover your values, engage in effective communication instead of ineffective communication. This is the foundation that you will use to build the University of Us.

- When a couple is united intimately, they can build infinitely

- A vision helps us to get on the same page and walk together in moving our lives towards the place that God has called us to.

- Connect with mentors that can hold you accountable to your vision. Tell them what you both want to achieve. Be honest with them about your progressions and regressions.

Becoming Intimate Life-Builders

1. Download the values exercise from notjustroommates.org and complete it

2. Complete the vision and values exercise with your spouse

3. Compare your top priorities and values

4. Using effective communication discuss how you can meet these needs and create plans to carry them out

5. Find and connect with mentors who can hold you accountable

For Reflection:

- What has God shown you to be the vision of your marriage? What type of legacy so you want to leave?

Chapter 6

Divided We Fall

"Every kingdom divided against itself is headed for destruction, and no city or house divided against itself will stand."

~ *Matthew 12:25 (HCSB)*

Imagine if you were sitting inside of your dream home. It's a beautiful home with five bedrooms, three bathrooms, and a huge backyard. Let's throw in huge flat screen TVs on the walls, a surround sound theater room, and bathrooms with heated floors. Add in the top-of-the-line furniture and a three-car garage. I'm talking about an amazing home with green acres. Imagine something HGTV would give away as a special prize.

Now imagine that a husband and a wife receive their own wrecking ball machines. Out of the blue they let the wrecking balls rip. Destroying one room after another. There's madness and anarchy on the inside of the home. The children are confused as to why it's happening. Their family and loved ones are shocked by the demolition of their vision. As you imagine the demolition of this dream home, what goes through your mind? I'd say, it's sad to see a dream home destroyed by its own owners for any reason.

Oftentimes, couples will sit in my office and I can see from the outside that they have everything that a marriage is made of. They have all the right ingredients, but mixed them up improperly. They love each other and are a beautiful family. They married one another to build their dream home. Most of the people I counsel share a relationship with God. Yet they're fighting against themselves, and with wrecking-ball intensity smashing it down. If your home is collapsing, we must find where you are divided as a couple.

Fighting instead of uniting

Imagine if a football team is lined up on offense. Their focus is to score and make it across the goal line. In the game of football there is a defense that's lined up and determined to stop the offense. Picture the defense in formation and ready to shut the offense down. But before the snap of the ball, the offensive players on the same team yelled and argued with one another.

In a fit of rage they broke from their formation and fought one another. I mean, they're going at it. It turns into an all-out, self-destructive fight. Regardless of what caused the fight or what they were fighting for, we can all agree that they've fallen short of teamwork. Even worse for them, the defense didn't even have to do anything to shut them down. Why? Because they were too busy fighting instead of uniting. They caved in on themselves, just like the dream home.

This is what it looks like when a team is divided. Husbands and wives must be on each other's team. There is no room for anger, hatred, or bitterness. There's no room for contention with the overall vision and plan of the home. What would it take for your family to get a shared vision?

I can't tell you how many times I found myself divided against my wife. There were moments when I wanted to do things my way or she could take the highway. There were times when she wanted to do things her way and we would bump heads. In fact, this was one of the main reasons early in our marriage we contemplated a divorce.

We couldn't see eye to eye on basic decisions. No matter what the subject, we couldn't seem to agree on how to get things done.

She and I both wanted what was best for the home but envisioned separate pathways to get the job done. I didn't understand her personality, and she didn't understand mine.

We were so passionate about getting it right that we would fight to defend our perspectives and in doing so, we would harm one another. When you think about that, it's counterproductive. We want the right answer because we want to help the person we love. But we defend our position so aggressively that we enter attack mode and it becomes a fight to be right.

Have you and your spouse come to where it's a fight to be right rather than a fight to unite? If so, I encourage you to remember that your spouse comes before your plans. The plans are for the benefit of you both. Differing opinions isn't worth dividing the home!

Take a Walk before you Talk and Pray before you Say

An angry man stirs up strife, And a hot-tempered man abounds in transgression. ~ Proverbs 29:22 (NASB95)

There's nothing wrong with taking a break before continuing a discussion. Do whatever it takes to avoid hurting a person over proving a point. If you're not walking in self-control, you might say something in anger that'll cause more damage than good. Take the time to pray and release the tension. You don't want to stir up strife or instigate a fight. A hot temper can cause confrontation that leads to sinful actions. Walk it off, and release the stress to God.

I don't want you to assume I'm saying to hold your thoughts inside. I'm saying that there are right attitudes, times, and places for discussion rather than bringing up issues at will. If you hold in your thoughts, you'll eventually explode or implode. This isn't healthy for you or your spouse.

An angry heart in the heat of the moment is a sign of being offended. Holding onto offense is never a good thing. When God created human beings, he didn't design us to hold grudges. Grudges and resentment permitted in your heart are house dividers. It's okay to take a break if things get heated, but I'm not suggesting going into hiding or denying.

God Didn't Design for us to be Dishonest

What I mean by that is that if I don't tell you what's on my mind, I rob you of the whole truth. I'm not being honest. I'll give you an example: my wife would see me upset or distant. Picture me with an all-out pout for whatever reason I'm upset or discouraged. My face and body language, or lack of any language, would give away the truth.

She'd ask me, "What's wrong?" I'd reply, "Nothing," or, "I've got a lot on my mind." In this moment I'm denying her the truth and deflecting a transparent conversation when she's trying to bring a resolution. She's reaching out for intimacy and I'm shutting her out. This is division.

Differing opinions should not divide the home!

Most times, I'm frustrated with her because of something she said or didn't do. But I wasn't giving her a chance to defend her side before I rendered a guilty verdict against her. I judged her actions and condemned her to be cut off from honest communication.

This is where the enemy of our souls sits back and laughs. Satan doesn't have to do anything in this scenario to bring down the house. The defense sits back and watches the offense tear itself apart. We are divided against ourselves, and divided we fall.

Matthew 12:25 (HCSB): 25 Knowing their thoughts, He told them: "Every kingdom divided against itself is headed for destruction, and no city or house divided against itself will stand.

These examples could go on all day long, but hopefully I've communicated the point. When I shut her out I prejudged her actions and condemned her to the silent treatment. I permitted the separation of my home instead of unity. I'm investing in our marriage's failure and withdrawing from its success. Divided we fall. United the house will stand.

Communicate honestly with your spouse, but with grace and mercy. The time you speak with them and how you speak with them must be with unity as the goal. Try to strive to be honest about how you felt when something was said or done that rubbed you the wrong way. Still, pick your battles. Some things you should just let slide. Yet when the moment comes to confront an issue, do so at the right time.

Chapter Summary

- If your home is collapsing, we must find where you are divided as a couple

- There's no room for contention with the overall vision and plan of the home

- Don't be so passionate about being right that you fight to defend your perspectives

- Learn how to walk in self-control. If you have a temper, walk it off-release the stress to God

- When confronting an issue, do so at the right time

Becoming Intimate Life-Builders

1. Identify the areas that your home is collapsing. After praying, write them down and discuss with your spouse

2. Identify the areas that you are holding grudges and resentment again the spouse. Prayerfully pursue time and method to discuss with spouse in love

3. The next time your spouse offends you, release it and then discuss with your spouse in the same day

For Reflection:

- Ask the Holy Spirit to reveal areas where you are not being transparent with your spouse. Prayerfully pick your battles and meet with your spouse to discuss in a safe emotional environment

Chapter 7

The Dirty S Word

There's a myth that must be busted before we can move forward in pursuit of intimacy. False teaching and womanizers paint an ugly picture of a woman's role in the home. So let's get something straight from the start: From a biblical perspective, wives should submit to their husbands.

Yet this word submit gets interpreted as a wife should become her husband's personal slave; that she is subservient and a doormat for her husband to walk on.

This is a load of garbage! That isn't even close to what Paul the apostle had in mind when he penned Ephesians 5. This definitely isn't a reflection on the heart of God.

For the sake of clarity, victory, and freedom, I'd like to discuss with you this dirty word submit and wash away its guilty stain. Instead of using a more traditional translation of this infamous controversy, we're reading from The Message version; let's check it out:

Ephesians 5:22–24 (The Message): Wives, understand and support your husbands in ways that show your support for Christ. The husband provides leadership to his wife the way Christ does to his church, not by domineering but by cherishing. So just as the church submits to Christ as he exercises such leadership, wives should likewise submit to their husbands.

Do you feel a little of the dirt washing away? This verse is not advocating the worship of your spouse as Lord. It is encouraging wives to respect their husbands as to the Lord. You show respect to your own husband as a service to Christ. This doesn't mean that if your husband tells you to bark like a big dog and hop on one leg, you obey his command. God is saying that a woman should honor her man and in doing so, establishes order within the home.

If you think about it, this makes sense. Any Christian woman that's a representative of the marriage covenant who would dishonor her husband is a misrepresentation of the covenant. The covenant says you're one with your man. Why would someone disrespect themselves or treat themselves with contempt? Wouldn't someone want to receive honor and respect from their fellow man towards themselves? Shouldn't a husband at the least want a wife who respects him. Aretha Franklin has a hit song about r-e-s-p-e-c-t. Let's sing it within our marriages.

As you can see in the above translation, the goal is to support and understand your husband. What's the opposite of that? To be unsupportive and to ignore him. I can guarantee you this; men need honor. They want support and understanding. Someone to cheer them on and be in their corner throughout life's battles. Can you be that woman for him?

As your husband is making efforts to lead the home, he will make mistakes. Sometimes he may not behave that respectable! In these moments, he doesn't need your supporting side to be thrown out the window. That's when you've got to remember that you didn't marry a perfect man. Please create a space for grace in your expectations of him. You may want him to be more expressive, and to let you into his thoughts in moments of stress. He will never let you in if he has experienced that when you get in there you tear him apart with your criticisms of his mistakes.

Women want security, and to express feelings through conversations and deliberation. Most men go into fix-it mode when their backs are against the wall. Sometimes we don't want to talk it out and share feelings. So, it appears as if men shut down or are doing nothing. Please understand that in most men who are trying their best, they are just as concerned as you are. But they don't want to appear weak or incapable. When the money is funny and critical deadlines are approaching, he wants a solution, but might be stressed about how to make it work. And if he can't make it work, he feels like a failure. In these difficult times, he doesn't need your criticism, he needs your support and respect.

Submission doesn't mean you must do whatever he says or that your opinion is insignificant. This entire book is about having shared vision and agreement. It's about building your lives together. Your opinion is valued and should be expressed. Sit down with him at the University of Us and ask him how to approach him in moments of turmoil. Express to him what you need from him and how you feel when he goes into his cave of silence.

But how you deliver that opinion and when you discuss matters of the heart matters. Is it respectful of him as a man? When you speak with him, is it in a respectful tone? Is there an insult or sarcasm within your words? Do you treat him as you would a child? If so, you will push him away from the direction you desire.

The Key Verse That's Missed

What blows my mind about the word submission is that people think the word is so dirty that they don't want to use it. What's ironic about it is that people harp on this word being used of women, but if you read the chapter in its entirety, it's about mutual submission. Submission isn't exclusive to women. Locate the word submit in each verse and the order in which it is mentioned:

Ephesians 5:21–25 (NLT): 21 And further, submit to one another out of reverence for Christ. 22 For wives, this means submit to your husbands as to the Lord. 23 For a husband is the head of his wife as Christ is the head of the church. He is the Savior of his body, the church. 24 As the church submits to Christ, so you wives should submit to your husbands in everything. 25 For husbands, this means love your wives, just as Christ loved the church. He gave up his life for her (emphasis added by me).

Notice how the word submit is used in verse 21 for both the husband and the wife! It's a mutual submission. Then Paul expresses how the submissions are demonstrated. People highlight the word on wives, but it's applicable to the husband as well. How we submit to one another is according to God's design of our greatest needs.

Verse 22 starts out: ." . . for the wives this means . . ." or she submits in this manner. Verse 25 says: ." . . For husbands this means . . ." You see, Christ has commissioned men to lead with love, and in doing so he meets the greatest need of the woman, security. Every wife wants to be loved sacrificially; that's her ultimate security.

On the other hand, every man equates love with honor. So the best way that a wife can serve her husband is through support or respect. How wives speak to their husbands when times are good determines their level of support. The same is true about how she treats her husband when the times are tough. This is a man's number one need. I think respect outranks sex, and that's saying something.

Submission is a two-way street. It's for both the husband and the wife. How we communicate and show that submission is different. This is because men and women are built with a different priority of needs. It's great if you support your husband when he's winning in life, but he needs you to cheer him on even when he's having a losing season.

Regardless of your gender, the principle of submission is required to agree. Give yourselves to one another as you submit your lives to the Lord.

Chapter Summary

- False teaching and womanizers paint an ugly picture of a woman's role in the home. For wives, submit should not be interpreted as being her husband's personal slave

- According to Ephesians 5:22-24. The goal is to support and understand your husband. Men need honor, they want support and understanding

- Remember, you didn't marry the perfect man, please create a space for grace in your expectations of him

- Submission doesn't mean you must do whatever he says or that your opinion is insignificant

- Sit down with him at the University of Us and ask him how to approach him in moments of turmoil. Express to him what you need from him and how you feel when he goes into his cave of silence

- Be cautious of how you deliver your opinion: is it respectful to him as a man, spoken in a respectful tone

- In Ephesians 5:21, Paul is directing the message of submission to the husband and the wife. Submission between spouses is to be mutual

- Men are commissioned by Christ to lead with love

- Every wife wants to be loved sacrificially; that's her ultimate security

Becoming Intimate Life-Builders

1. Wives- ask your husband the best way to approach him in moments of turmoil

2. Pray and ask your husband in what ways you can show him support and understanding

3. Remember that you didn't marry a perfect man. Look first to

give him space for grace when he gets it wrong

4. Husbands- Allow her to tell you what she needs and what she needs from you

5. Allow God to show you in what ways can you love her sacrificially

For Reflection:

- In what ways can you take your submission to one another to the next level?

Chapter 8

Covenant & Commitment

In some cultures, they celebrate a marriage ceremony built around a salt covenant.

Salt is a preservative and purifier that prevents decay and corruption. It's enduring, unchanging, and lasts a long time. Salt is a symbol of God's character and dependability.

So, the phrase "Covenant of Salt" is a picture of the everlasting nature of the covenant relationship between the children of God and our Creator. When entering into a Covenant of Salt, one party binds themselves to another in the highest loyalty and truthfulness, even suffering death rather than break the covenant. So a Covenant of Salt was never done haphazardly . . . it deserves serious respect.

Now a Marriage Salt Covenant does the same thing by asking the husband and wife to combine their grains of salt. Imagine the man and woman bringing a pound of salt granules. They then take from their individual pouches and combine the salt into one new pouch. Their covenant with each other cannot be broken unless they can each retrieve their own grains of salt from the unified salt mixture. Since this is not possible, it is a symbol of an unbreakable covenant and vow of eternal love.

Your marriage should endure, and you both should be inseparable! What's amazing is that your union is a spiritual reality. God has merged you two together; you've just got to catch up in the natural realm with what has taken place in the spiritual realm.

My wife and I came to a point in our marriage where we took the threat of divorce off the table, declaring that divorce was not an option. We aligned our lives with the covenant we made before God. Our lives are bound in a lifelong commitment. So why not have the best lifelong relationship we could attain? We bought into marriage God's way and it's worked wonderfully for us. It can work for you as well, if you do it God's way!

Matthew 19:3–8 (YLT): 3 And the Pharisees came near to him, tempting him, and saying to him, 'Is it lawful for a man to put away his wife for every cause?' 4 And he answering said to them, 'Did ye not read, that He who made them, from the beginning a male and a female made them, 5 and said, For this cause shall a man leave father and mother, and cleave to his wife, and they shall be--the two--for one flesh? 6 so that they are no more two, but one flesh; what therefore God did join together, let no man put asunder.' 7 They say to him, 'Why then did Moses command to give a roll of divorce, and to put her away?' 8 He saith to them—'Moses for your stiffness of heart did suffer you to put away your wives, but from the beginning it hath not been so.

Notice Jesus goes so far in verse 5–6 as saying they are one flesh. That's a stretch, right? She's a female and I'm male, that's different flesh, right? This one flesh represents ownership. Now, we might not like that idea, but that's what takes place in a marriage. The man has ownership of the woman, and the woman has owner-ship of the man. That's why life insurance policies or tax benefits work the way they do; they acknowledge the two as one. Some-times a wife may sign in place of her husband being there, and so forth.

There is another view of this principle when we consider sex: two bodies merge as one. I don't have to get too graphic for us to see the picture of two bodies joined as one during intercourse. What's amazing about this is that new life can come forth out of this union. That's a powerful picture of the strength of unity.

Jesus said what God has joined together, no one should divide. The corrupt religious leaders of Jesus' day decided they'd count-

er Jesus' leadership by bringing up their famous leader M
practice of permitting divorce. Jesus responds that Mose
the custom of divorce due to the hardness of the people's .
towards their spouses. But then Jesus states that this wasn't God's
best from the beginning. He's referring to the first marriage in the
Garden of Eden between Adam and Eve.

There are so many points of discussion here, but the main one
I'll make first is that divorce isn't God's best for us. There are
extreme cases where it's necessary. But I've discovered that most
people who dissolve the salt do so because of a failure to overcome
their areas of discord.

Strength in Unity

I created a CD entitled "Not Just Roommates" (available for download on iTunes). The title track says in the chorus, "You're not my
enemy, so I'll be good to you and you be good to me." Too often,
husbands and wives are at war with one another.

Angry, bitter, contemptuous, and dissatisfied. Look at the
words in the last sentence; consider each one as if it were an attitude. How can a house stay strong and unified when those attitudes
are the attributes that govern the actions? Someone's got to love as
Jesus has commanded us to do.

*Ephesians 4:32 (NLT): Instead, be kind to each other, tender-
hearted, forgiving one another, just as God through Christ has
forgiven you.*

Now my purpose in presenting those passages is not to condemn, but to compel you to walk in your God-given identity. As
a child of the King, you and I are to respond to God's instructions
regardless of what others do around us, including our spouse.

It's easy to love someone when they're being nice; not so easy
when they're not. Still, loving the "unlovable" is not impossible. It
amazes me as a pastor how many people will be Christian in con-
fession until their spouse treats them in a manner that's not pleas-

ing to them. Christian and faith-filled—until it's time to believe God to strengthen them to be good to their life partner when times are tough.

Hey, you can still do all things through Christ who strengthens you! Does your mate have the power to nullify the influence of the Holy Spirit in your life? If so, that means you've placed your spouse in a position that only God can fill; mistake!

Your spouse may do or say things that offend you, but you must release the offenses of your mate. You must stay Christ-like no matter what. If you're expecting perfection from your spouse 24/7 then you're setting yourself up for disappointment.

Every marriage needs grace and mercy, as God has given us grace and mercy. He accepts us as his children, knowing we'd have flaws and so in advance he forgives. That's a good policy to live by; forgive your spouse, and the contempt and anger goes away.

There can be no unity where there's hatred, bitterness, or resentment.

Why? You'll despise the person you're with and seek to relieve yourself of what you believe to be the source of your pain. But in the marriage covenant, you two are one. So, if your spouse is struggling in an area, you're being affected by it. Ask yourself how can you bring about healing, restoration, or love through the hurt? No matter what, forgive and be free.

When you take a healthy man and a healthy woman you get a healthy marriage. Didn't say perfect man or woman, but a healthy one. When there's habitual sin or spiritual bondage individually, it affects the whole. A gambling problem affects the budget for the entire home. A porn addiction will destroy trust and create unrealistic expectations within a marriage. Anger and quick tempers that aren't healed will erode a relationship. There are plenty of ministries out there to help with spiritual strongholds . . . get the help you need as soon as you can. In the meantime, grace has to fill the place.

Love has to cover your spouse's sins or imperfections. You're not out to accuse one another. You watch each other's back for life. That's a house that'll walk in unity. A home where a wife honors her husband and the husband loves his wife through their words and actions—that's a home that'll be blessed.

Psalm 133:1–3 (NLT): 1 How wonderful and pleasant it is when brothers live together in harmony! 2 For harmony is as precious as the anointing oil that was poured over Aaron's head, that ran down his beard and onto the border of his robe. 3 Harmony is as refreshing as the dew from Mount Hermon that falls on the mountains of Zion. And there the Lord has pronounced his blessing, even life everlasting.

The Lord will add a blessing on the man and woman striving to keep harmony. It takes work to stay on the same page!

A word of caution on your journey: don't look into the home of another couple thinking that everything magically works together. Stop looking at movies thinking that there's something magical that you're missing out on. Every real relationship will experience its difficulties, but if you both fight to stay together, God will bless you.

The blessing of God is right there in the midst of your harmonious home. The salt is mixed. You're now bone of bone and flesh of flesh. I believe God will anoint or empower your marriage to conquer every attack that comes against it.

Keep Hope Alive!

You may say to yourself that there's no hope for your spouse from a spiritual standpoint. But every man or woman of God that you respect has a past. Every married couple you look up to has a story. God has to develop and mature them as well. They've got their flaws. Their spouse has had to endure turbulent times with them on their journey. So don't be fooled by the illusion that your marriage is the only one with problems. You're not alone in having to work at keeping your marriage together.

You may believe God for things to improve in your family. Praying he will become a spiritual leader, or hoping she overcomes a spiritual bondage? Keep on believing and remain patient. As you both apply the principles in this book and work at it, things will get better. Remember that some of our greatest transformations come through our greatest tests.

When you clean your skin, you use soap and a towel to scrub. Sometimes God's process to purge the problem requires pain. So stick with your spouse and strive to keep unity through the scrub.

Live Peaceably Whenever Possible

Romans 12:17–18 (NKJV): 17 Repay no one evil for evil. Have regard for good things in the sight of all men. 18 If it is possible, as much as depends on you, live peaceably with all men.

I encourage you to connect with a marriage ministry in a local church. If you're not the church-going type, please know that a healthy church won't bite. Google or ask around about a healthy Christian church near you, and get there.

At the Crossroads Church in Fort Worth, Texas where I pastor, our marriage ministry is Not Just Roommates. I think one of the greatest benefits of the connect groups we offer are the group discussions. You'll discover others who go through similar situations. But not only that, you'll discover that they overcome, and they give great advice.

Treasure, Favor, and Anointing

Proverbs 18:22 (NLT): The man who finds a wife finds a treasure, and he receives favor from the Lord.

As we check this passage of wisdom out we find a lot of juicy nuggets. To the man, you receive God's favor because of that treasure of a woman in your life! You may say, "She doesn't seem that great." That's your problem right there. God didn't call you to be her judge. You're the winner of an amazing treasure from the stash of heaven.

God says she's a treasure, and you'd do well to agree with him on this one. Speak positively about her regardless of what you see. Don't allow Satan to interpret her value to you. You'll adopt a negative image by the time he's done with you. Image ties into imagination. You can imagine her to be your trash instead of your treasure. Your imagination inspired by Satan gives you a poor interpretation, and your inspiration to love her is removed. Don't believe the hype. She's a good woman, and you've discovered a great treasure! Don't lose her.

God favors you even though you and I know you don't deserve it! Who better to give grace than one who's in desperate need of it first? Come on, men, do you need grace? The obvious answer is yes!

God himself has given you grace; how about giving her the same? How about you cover your wife and her flaws instead of being critical of them all? Share the favor of God on your life with your wife.

In the past, I've had moments where I embarrassed my wife in front of people. My conduct was sarcastic or cold towards her. It was wrong, but it was because of the way I imagined her to be in that moment. I saw her negatively, and so I treated her poorly. In all actuality, she's the most beautiful woman in the world. It comforts me to know that she's the mother of my children and the biggest supporter of all I am as a man.

I'm grateful for what we are now, but I was an idiot and almost lost her. Don't be the idiot that almost loses your treasure. The grass looks greener on the other side, but it's a lie. Satan is a master manipulator, and he hates marriage. He puts in work to twist our perspectives against our mates. Don't be fooled into giving up your good thing for the lie of an illusion.

Chapter Summary

- When entering into a covenant of salt, one party binds themselves to another in the highest loyalty and truthfulness, even suffering death rather than break the covenant

- A man and wife become one flesh in marriage. One flesh represents ownership. The man has ownership of the woman and the woman has ownership of the man

- A blessed home is one where a wife honors her husband and the husband loves his wife through their words and actions

- In Proverbs 18:22, the wife is described by God as a treasure. Husbands, agree with Him by speaking positively about her regardless of what you see. Don't allow satan to interpret her value to you. Cover your wife and her flaws

Becoming Intimate Life-Builders

1. Take a few moments to reflect on your marriage covenant with your spouse and discuss what it means to you

2. Establish a daily practice of releasing your mate from their offenses

3. Look for opportunities to bring healing, restoration, and love through hurt in your marriage

For Reflection:

- In what areas do you need to establish/reinforcement peace and unity?

Resources

- Not Just Roommates by Sean Reed (available on ITunes and Google Play)

Chapter 9

Show Me State

I'm from St. Louis, Missouri, better known as "the show me state." At some point, spouses will arrive at a place called "show me." It's great that meaningful conversations will begin and plans are created after reading this book. Then the moment comes where it's like . . . show me.

Many people are in a state called "show me." Show me with your actions that you love, respect, or are committed to the marriage. Present evidence of a commitment to the plans we make together, some assurance of real change.

You are a spiritual being with emotions and a physical body. Your spouse can't see your spirit, but they can experience your emotions and spiritual intentions through your body. Your body's actions communicate what your mind, will, and emotions desire to express. Sometimes, our actions speak louder than our words.

Your physical body is what your spouse sees and interacts with in life. They can't read your mind, but they may misinterpret it. Your communication is both verbal and nonverbal. To develop trust and intimacy within your marriage, put works to the words.

Living with leftovers

Don't leave your spouse living with leftovers. You may be fatigued from work or frustrated because you're bogged down by the weight of financial burdens. Do you retreat under pressure? Your spouse may receive this communication as a message of shutting them out. They can't read your mind. They may be clueless to what's going on in your spirit. But you can fix this. You can become a great communicator of your thoughts and clarify your actions.

Another thing that helps with this as well is that if your spouse shuts you out, don't be so quick to take it personally. Everything they do isn't an attack against you. A mood swing isn't a punch to your face. It may be the residue of a frustrating day that needs to be rinsed away by your grace. A foot massage may be in order in the home instead of reciprocating a bad attitude. Remember, your spouse isn't your enemy; you're partners. If they fall, try to pick them up before you cast them down.

Show your spouse how important they are to you. Where are the cards, handwritten poetry, or the flowers? What about giving your spouse your undivided attention when they want to talk to you? How about special lingerie or a hot bubble bath prepared for them when they get home? The list can go on and on, but what you'll find is that a little intentionality can go a long way. What I've discovered is that I usually perform what I intentionally plan.

Many times we want our marriage to work. But we think that magic dust from heaven will fall and transform all the flaws in our marriage. It doesn't happen like that. God gives us the grace to get it together. We can walk in the strength of that grace and get to working. Nothing can stop you from doing your part, but you.

Let me ask you; what are you going to do this day to communicate love to your spouse? Just being alive in the same room with them or going to work won't cut it. You'd do that if you weren't with them. How will you uniquely show your love today? What action can you put behind the "I love you"?

After your spouse has opened up within the values blueprint, you've got to try to produce a result. Would you get a check if you never showed up for work? Show up and fulfill your end of the deal. Then, after you bring action, the reaction is a payday. I'm not trying to reduce marriage to a work negotiation, but we get returns as we make investments. As your spouse sees and experiences the fruit of your love, you'll get a harvest of reciprocity.

Once you factor in work time, traffic time, time for the children, and time getting dressed, you may discover that you have little time with your spouse. What does that leftover time look like with your spouse? Is it quality time? What is the atmosphere like when you and your spouse spend time together? If you become intentional and execute a plan for the leftover time with your spouse, you can make it a passionate time. You can make it an intimate, life-building time.

Why live the rest of your life as roommates? Why not live in a fun environment filled with spontaneity? You can change the atmosphere in your home today. How can you change the atmosphere? Intentionality. When you become intentional about meeting your spouse's needs in a manner they've communicated at the University of Us, you become the ultimate servant.

This day you can make a quality investment in your spouse. Deposit an investment that reflects your heart for them. You love them in your heart and in your mind, this is the truth. Will you prove this through your actions on a daily basis? Most times women are frustrated because men won't take initiative. Many men are frustrated with a lack of consistent, passionate sex. How do we fix this? Intentionality.

In the back-and-forth pendulum of disappointment and unmet expectations, the marriage growth may be stunted. So, if you want your marriage to grow, don't just talk, but talk, plan, and act. Show them you love them.

Chapter Summary

- Many people are in a state called "show me." Show me with your actions that you love, respect, or are committed to the marriage. Your spouse can't see your spirit, but they can experience your emotions and spiritual intentions through your body.

- To develop trust and intimacy within your marriage, put works to the words

- Don't leave your spouse living with leftovers. Show your spouse that they are important to you

- You will perform what you intentionally plan. Magic dust from heaven will not fall and transform all the flaws in your marriage

- Change the atmosphere of your home through intentionality. When you become intentional about meeting your spouse's needs in a manner they've communicated, you become the ultimate servant

Becoming Intimate Life-Builders

1. Using the lists established from Chapter 5 (values and vision), discuss and plan intentional ways to execute if this has not already been done

2. Identify investments that you can make into your marriage

3. Plan ways to serve your spouse with the best of your time and energy

For Reflection:

- In what ways can you deposit an investment into your spouse? Think about how frequently and when you can make these investments

Chapter 10

It's Our Time

Life is just like a fog. It's not from the ground, but somehow a cloud is here. It's like a fragmented piece of an atmospheric cloud from heaven that came down to cover the earth. That's similar to a human being's life experience.

We're gifts of God, made in his image and likeness. Children of the Heavenly Father, placed on this earth for a short time. That time can be 120 years or less. No matter how long or short, it's all but a vapor, just a moment in God's eyes, just a small piece of an eternal puzzle. But the decisions made will produce dramatic and eternal consequences. Our decisions leave lasting impacts on the people surrounding us and on the generations that'll come after our time.

So if you and I are like the fog, now is our time. We've made it to earth! Traveled from an idea in the mind of God the Creator to the hands of a doctor. Then to the nurse . . . to the heat tray, and then to the parents. We are hungry and focused on one thing in that moment: it's not finance, not clothing, but it's food and warmth. The warmth of the home we'd once known inside of our mother.

Instinct kicks in. We've never latched on to a breast or bottle, but today, it will happen. I will eat because I'm programmed to fight for my survival. Preprogrammed to survive and thrive.

We are preprogrammed to fight for survival and experience life. Why? I believe it's because we come from the mind of God, the

Eternal Creator and Source of life itself. Our spirit is made in the image and likeness of God. That doesn't mean that God has curly hair and green eyes. It's not his physical features, but the spiritual ones we show.

God designed each of us to reflect an attribute of his ability. He embedded in our hearts a sense of purposefulness. Our desire to live forever results from originating from an eternal God. God lives forever . . . the good news here is that we will live forever one day. Yet this physical body has an expiration date.

Try as we might to make it last forever, it won't. Botox, elixirs, lifts, tucks, implants, diets, and surgeries can preserve the inevitable for so long. It will come to an end, but why? It's because this physical body is a cocoon, if you will, and at the resurrection or the Rapture we'll receive a new body that'll last forever. At that moment the need to be physically eternal will match the intensity of a deep-seated celestial desire within us. For now we must face the reality that time is a temporary reality created by God to govern our affairs in this life.

What we do with the gift of time is important. One day we will stand before our Maker to account for what we accomplished in this life. Do you want to stand and say you gave your all with the time you had to live? That you lived each day to the fullest. That you made the most of every day of every year given to you. I hope that at the end of your life you can say you made the most of your time.

With that in mind, I encourage every couple reading this book to act upon the wisdom of God's instructions. Every day is a gift from God to live life on purpose. To give excellent service to our family, starting with our spouse. You can either live in victory or misery. You and your spouse can choose to go all in building your dreams together.

Your marriage can show the love of God to the entire world. When you live with this sense of urgency you'll be able to stand before God knowing you lived each day with a sense of purpose. That you made the most of your time.

The Sum of the Line

As a pastor, I've had the privilege of marrying couples, christening children, and baptizing believers, and every once in a while, the honor of eulogizing funerals, or what I like to call home-goings. Home-goings can be tough days of ministry.

For those who die in the Lord it's a time of rejoicing, but it's a time of sadness as well. Although we know we'll see them again, years for us are long, and the grief of missing that person is hard to bear.

In those moments of bereavement, I think that we are like dazed boxers in the ring of life. We've taken a hard blow that has us dazed to a point of disorientation. Then the trainer snaps the tube of smelling salts underneath our noses and it awakens us. Snaps us back to a state of consciousness.

Home-goings and funerals can snap us back to the reality of how temporal this journey is, how fragile this vapor of a life can be. We can be here one moment and gone the next. Gradually the days and years pass from those moments of eternal clarity . . . TV shows, movies, Facebook, and the hustle of life once again get us caught up in the daze.

The fight for survival kicks in as we try to elongate our time. Soon thereafter, the reality of the next life again gets washed away. This causes us to take the days for granted, and we forget about the severity of each second. We might lose sight of the reality that each individual day of good success leads up to a culmination of a life well-lived.

Is it Worth it to Waste a Day?

In light of the preciousness of time, is it worth it to waste a day angry, in bitterness, or at war with your spouse? Consider the backdrop of eternity and ask yourself if it's worth it to give your joy away today. Are the frustrations troubling our minds worth tolerating?

I know they didn't take out the trash, but is that worth giving away your joy for a week? When you consider how precious each day is, you may realize that the weight of what your spouse has done isn't eternally heavy. With this frame of mind, you'll find it easier to let petty things go.

All of us, I presume, have taken a walk through a graveyard. We've laid eyes on a gravestone. Some show the birth date and death date under the name of the departed. In between those numbers is a dash. That dash, that little line between birth and death, is the sum of a lifetime. It's the reality of what we've accomplished as human beings.

For some people the sum of that line will represent the years they changed their family, community, and world for the better. The world will remember them and will "miss them when they're gone."

For others that dash will represent a life poorly spent, with no impactful legacy. It'll represent dreams and potential wasted because they didn't maximize the time for whatever reason. The sum of their line will represent nothing more than wasted time.

This can't be your life! This cannot be your marriage. Why settle for the ordinary when you can live the extraordinary? You get the choice to live life on purpose. Your marriage must be more than a partnership for tax breaks and joint income. Your marriage must accomplish more than staying together for the sake of the kids.

You were created to represent God in this world in a powerful way. Your time on earth cannot be wasted in mediocrity and procrastination. We must maximize the time we get to carry out the dreams and visions that God has given us as intimate life-builders.

Remember, God created time, but it will not be around forever. God will do away with time and then we'll experience eternity-life without time. My point here is this our dash is to God and humanity what we believed, what we stood for and valued. The sum of the line is the values we lived, and that determines the eternal legacy we'll leave in this world.

That's heavy stuff, I know! It's a lot of pressure to perform while on this planet; but we've got help along the way. God is tapping into the eternal elements within us and is resuscitating deep within us our awareness for something more than average. He's luring your marriage to something greater than a decaying existence. He's calling us to an extraordinary life that'll have eternal resonation.

Chapter Summary

- What we do with the gift of time is important. Your marriage can show the love of God to the entire world

- In light of the preciousness of time, don't waste a day living in anger, bitterness or at war with your spouse

- Maximize the time in your marriage to carry out the dreams and visions that God has given you as intimate life-builders

- The sum of your years lived reflects the values you lived and that determines the eternal legacy you'll leave in this world

- God is calling us to an extraordinary life that'll have eternal resonation.

Becoming Intimate Life-Builders

1. Implement the plans that you put into place from Chapter 9. Overcome fallacies in thinking, I.e. "When the time is right/ circumstances are more favorable"

2. Prioritize walking in joy- consider the backdrop of eternity when your spouse offends you and just brush it off. It's not worth wasting a day

3. Take some time and reflect what you would want your eulogy to be. What would the sum of your life say about you?

For Reflection:

- In what ways can you spend your time to be more fulfilling? Are you living life to its fullest? If not, why?

Chapter 11

Procrastin The Assassin

I'm not talking about you, but some people are flat-out lazy. They want great results out of life but aren't willing to put forth worthwhile effort. There comes a time in our lives when talk and intentions must be converted into action. Results and laziness will never be friends. Procrastination is the assassination of our destinations. Why? Because procrastin is an assassin. Laziness in your marriage will kill your dreams. Listen to what King Solomon has to say about laziness.

Proverbs 13:4 (NLT): 4 Lazy people want much but get little, but those who work hard will prosper.

Your spouse shouldn't live at the altar of broken promises. Throughout my time in ministry, I've noticed that couples know the proper action steps. Still they aren't intense enough when it comes down to executing a plan.

Hard work in marriage commits to follow through on meeting the needs of your spouse. At the University of Us, you dedicate yourself to learning your spouse's values, needs, and desires. You lovingly partner with your friend to make your house a happy home.

Now, I'm not just saying to be busy for the sake of feeling like you're accomplishing something. I want you to develop well-thought-out plans that happen. You can't expect great results without taking effective action to achieve them. You can uproot procrastin the assassin through diligence.

Proverbs 19:24 (NLT): 24 Lazy people take food in their hand but don't even lift it to their mouth.

Isn't this sad when you consider the reality of Solomon's statement? It means you see all the proper nourishment for a healthy marriage, but won't ingest it. All the resources and wisdom are present to build an intimate partnership, but you refuse to get it, ingest it, and process it. A lazy spouse will starve the marriage to death, and the consequences are fatal.

Decide today on your part to be diligent. Diligence is the opposite of laziness.

Proverbs 12:27 (NLT): 27 Lazy people don't even cook the game they catch, but the diligent make use of everything they find.

The diligent people who are reading this book will make use of the wisdom they receive. Things will prosper in your relationship. Your family's dreams will become realities because you put in the work to get the results.

Things to Remember!

You have a choice to control your actions. At no point in your relationship do you have power over your spouse's actions. Please release them to God. Whatever actions they take with the time they get on this earth are their decision.

True, you are affected by their successes and failures. But you can't fix other people. You can only better yourself. The longer you invest your precious time trying to micromanage them, you miss out on your personal obedience to Christ.

Please remember that you and I aren't God. We can't control people. What's more interesting about controlling others is that God doesn't even control people. He's given us the freedom to choose in this world. The sooner we release people to God, the sooner we can be diligent as the person he's created us to be.

Mirrors for the Hearers

James 1:22–24 (HCSB): 22 But be doers of the word and not hearers only, deceiving yourselves. 23 Because if anyone is a hearer of the word and not a doer, he is like a man looking at his own face in a mirror. 24 For he looks at himself, goes away, and immediately forgets what kind of man he was.

When God reveals truth to you, it's like he's pulling out a mirror to show you what he wants to change. He's not trying to nitpick. God wants what's best for us, and sometimes that means removing something that's harmful to our health. He gives us a choice to hear his wisdom. He supplies truth just as a good parent supplies food. Your Heavenly Father wants to feed you nourishment for your betterment.

If he gives us instructions to follow that we forget, we deceive ourselves. If we walk away from godly instructions and refuse to do what's revealed, we revert to the same level of dysfunction. Don't you want to continue to grow? Do you want your marriage to achieve continued success? Then I encourage you to allow God to teach his wisdom to you.

Upon receiving his wisdom, just do it! Don't procrastinate what you need to do in this life that God has given you. Each second that ticks away is another opportunity to live the life you've dreamed of. It won't just fall into your lap; you must be diligent, and go get it.

Procrastination due to Fear

Some of us don't want to fail. We may strive for perfection, or we hate rejection. After being hurt in marriage, it's hard to try again. So we delay while our desires are denied.

But I'd rather try and fail than not try at all. We have very little time in this world and we must make the most of it. I'm reminded of Jesus walking on the water and then asking the disciples to join him in defying the natural elements.

Matthew 14:25–33 (NLT): 25 About three o'clock in the morning Jesus came toward them, walking on the water. 26 When the disciples saw him walking on the water, they were terrified. In their fear, they cried out, "It's a ghost!" 27 But Jesus spoke to them at once. "Don't be afraid," he said. "Take courage. I am here!" 28 Then Peter called to him, "Lord, if it's really you, tell me to come to you, walking on the water." 29 "Yes, come," Jesus said.

So Peter went over the side of the boat and walked on the water toward Jesus. 30 But when he saw the strong wind and the waves, he was terrified and began to sink. "Save me, Lord!" he shouted.

31 Jesus immediately reached out and grabbed him. "You have so little faith," Jesus said. "Why did you doubt me?" 32 When they climbed back into the boat, the wind stopped. 33 Then the disciples worshiped him. "You really are the Son of God!" they exclaimed.

Keep this in mind; God won't ask you to do something he's not already up to. He walks on the water first to show you that it's safe. Then, as you keep your eyes on him, he'll sustain you supernaturally. God has called you to defy the norm. To rise above what would usually drown you.

He is with you as you launch out into the deep, or as you "walk on the water." I'm asking you to try healthy communication with your spouse, again. Try forgiveness, again. Try working on your wealth together, again. Why try again? Well, it's not due to a change in your spouse. It's happening because of a change in you. Decide to be all that Jesus empowers you to be!

The journey of life is not designed to be played out as a soloist. Don't go at it alone. It takes divine intervention to keep a marriage. God is with you, and last I checked, he's El-Shaddai, which means: the God of more than enough. He's more than enough to supply your every need of every day.

Chapter Summary

- Procrastination is the assassination of our destinations. Laziness in your marriage will kill your dreams

- Your spouse shouldn't live at the altar of broken promises. Couples often know the proper action steps to take but aren't intense enough when it comes down to execution

- At the University of Us, you dedicate yourself to learning your spouse's values, needs and desires

- Upon receiving the wisdom of God, just do it! Don't procrastinate what you need to do in this life

- Don't be afraid to try again, it won't be because of a change in your spouse but because of a change in you

Becoming Intimate Life-Builders

1. Talk and intention must be converted into action. Begin to act on what you and your spouse have discussed. Completion is better than perfection

2. Look for ways to accomplish your goals using your current resources

3. Do it immediately- the longer you wait, the more likely you won't get to it

For Reflection:

- In what ways has Procrastin the Assassin stolen from you in your marriage. How can you take those things back?

Resource

- The Dream Book by Sean Reed

Chapter 12

See Your Priority

Did you know that you could discover my priorities through my bank account? If we pulled out my bank statements you could see my priorities. You'll see my cable bill, gym membership and clothing stores. You'd see my reoccurring payments to the mortgage, utility and phone companies. Observing each payment doesn't give you the whole picture, though. It's when you compare the investments of each transaction from my total income that you see what I value the most. When you compare them against one another, you can see my priorities.

In our marriage, our money was all over the place. It didn't reflect our core values. We were renting furniture with high interest rates and accruing debt from Payday Loans. Add to that high interest rate car notes and daily fast food stops, you could tell that we were broke because our vision was broken. We needed a financial plan built on our priorities and values.

One day my wife and I were purchasing life insurance for the first time. The agent selling us the insurance suggested that we read a book on finance. He left the book with us as a gift. He may have seen how jacked-up we were financially. We read it together, and discovered that we were in financial misery. We were digging a hole of debt, and we still had the shovel in our hands.

The starting point for us was to discover our values, passions, and purpose. We then determined to put our money where our lives where headed. For instance, we both loved supporting God's church. Spirituality is a top value for our home. So tithing was a must in our budget. We both had health as a major value, so we sacrificed the fast food for organic food. (And we sacrificed the money for that farm-raised bird.) Our children and family mean the world to us. So we sacrificed car payments for education and sports.

I think you all get the point. Prior to that paradigm-shifting moment, we modeled whatever lifestyles we adopted via TV, marketing, and life experiences. Over time, we embraced destructive behaviors that deterred us from our hearts' true priorities. We were working hard, but not smart. Everything changed when we aligned our time and treasure with our priorities.

Time Will Tell

You can tell my financial priorities with my bank statements, but you can tell my heart by tracking my time as well. Time will tell where my priorities are. There was a time when I'd work from 6:30 a.m. to 6:00 p.m. I'd get home and plop on the couch after a hard day's work, say a few words to my wife, and then head out the door to play basketball with friends. Upon returning home, I'd sit in front of the TV and either watch sports or play video games.

I can guarantee that my wife's needs for conversation and connection weren't being addressed. If you'd asked me at the time if this was improper behavior, I would've justified my actions. I can see now how I was neglecting our covenant. I wasn't committed to serving her, and I was destroying us.

Time will tell if your spouse and children are priorities to you. If you look through your schedule, will you discover that your family is in need of quality time with you? Please note that we aren't aiming for roommate status here! Being in the same room watching a TV screen together may not be intimate or productive time. Living under the same roof and saying good morning and good night isn't enough.

Time will tell if you are neglecting or nourishing your family.

I'm not suggesting here that you spend all day curled up on the couch together. I'm not saying to quit working and stare at each other until Jesus returns. My point here is that after all the hours spent in traffic, at the office, or the gym, your spouse needs you. They need your encouragement, flirting, attention, and sexuality.

What is time telling about you? Do your children take precedence over your spouse? If so, this is a mistake. It's a poor example for the children, and a detriment to your relationship. Your children should see your affection for one another. They need to see you engaging in healthy conversation. It'd be great if they could witness the adults apologizing to each other when you're in the wrong. Most of all, they need to see you both put one another first.

Date nights, dinner at the table as a family, and time at the park . . . that's quality time. Try to sync your schedules with your values. I get being overworked; but when your job is done with you, they'll lay you off without hesitation. Your family will be there with you till you die. Don't give a greater commitment to making money than making memories with your family.

You ever noticed that there's never been a U-Haul at a funeral? You can't take your possessions to heaven. If you spend your time pursuing possessions over your family then you're missing out, and your family is missing out on the joy of having you there.

I've gone to my kids' sporting events throughout their lives and seen children without their parents present to support them. It's a heartbreaking sight. Listen; I get that your job may not be flexible. But I've also seen people sacrifice time when their favorite artist is in town for a concert. People will stand in line for hours for the new release of a phone. I've seen people sit for hours in front of a television to watch their favorite team each week. People will spend their time on what they think is most important

I pray that time will tell that your family, next to God, is your highest priority. With the time you receive on this earth, make sure your actions show your heart. Your finances reflect your heart. What actions can you both take to align your actions, money, and time with your core values?

Chapter Summary

- You can tell your life priorities by tracking how your time is used

- Everything changes when we align our time and treasure with our priorities

- Being in the same room at the same time may not be intimate or productive time. Living under the same roof and saying good morning and good night isn't enough

- People will spend their time on what they think is most important. With the time you receive on this earth, make sure your actions show your heart

Becoming Intimate Life-Builders

1. Review how you can use your time and compare it to what you say your priorities are. Is this an accurate reflection of your heart

2. If your time and priorities don't align, work towards making them fit according to your priorities

3. Write out what it means to you to have your time align with your priorities. This will help motivate you during times of setbacks and discouragement

For Reflection:

- With the time you've received on this earth do your actions show your heart? What does the time you spend say about you?

Chapter 13

Set It or Forget It

Do you perform the things you plan? At the least, with a well-thought-out plan of action, you have a shot at being successful. If you want to graduate from roommate status, you can't be all talk and no walk. We've got to put legs to the plan at this point. As for my house, we must set it or forget it.

There's too much going on in our household to leave execution to chance. So Lanette and I plan what we intend to perform. There's a set time for us to look at the budget together. She likes to crunch the numbers initially by herself. She'll then set a time for us to meet to agree on the financial plan. When we don't have these financial meetings, the money madness will eventually manifest. Wealth building doesn't just happen. It takes a plan, and in marriage, financial success requires partnership.

At times we were so busy that we didn't carve out time for sex. Sometimes we were so busy that we neglected this essential area of connectivity. Look, I'm all for spontaneity in the bedroom, but sometimes you've got to set a time to get your love on.

I've often told the couples in our marriage ministry that roll-over-sex is a good thing. Rollover-sex is exactly as it sounds. There's no build up, no candles lit and no special music playing in the background. You just kind of . . . roll over and make it happen. It's sexual spontaneity.

Still, there's nothing like a prepared atmosphere. This requires time to get you all fresh and dressed for the occasion. You might have to make a date for a sexual commitment. Any parent out there with little ones knows that it takes time to get the kids asleep and the bedroom ready for action.

Side note: parents, lock your doors before intercourse. Otherwise your kids will get a shocking, life-altering and mind-warping experience. If you don't set that, they'll never forget it.

Sync Your Cal

Use the calendars on your phone. Technology gives us the ability to set reminders. We're at a point in history when a wristwatch can do the task of a desktop. Forgetting is almost not an option if you use daily reminders.

My wife loves flowers. I love buying them for her, but I'd forget to grab them on the way home. There came a point when I planned what I needed to perform. I set it so I wouldn't forget it. Those flowers earn me a lot of cool points, too.

Can you set aside a time during your week when you plan your romance? Sync your calendars to execute so you won't end up with another lame excuse. Don't leave it to chance. It doesn't make your gesture any less spontaneous or romantic. Most people meticulously planned their weddings. They thought through every detail because they wanted things to be perfect. But when it comes to life after the special day, they live average days. Why not make every day special? Please take this advice and make plans for the works of your hands.

Proverbs 16:3 (NLT): Commit your actions to the Lord, and your plans will succeed.

Your plans for finance, romance, or vacation can all be laid before the Lord in prayer. He will make your plans succeed. Pick your favorite search engine, and find ideas you can execute. Once you discover it, set it, or you might forget it. And then you'll regret it.

Chapter Summary

- If you want to graduate from roommate status, you can't be all talk and no walk. You must set it or else you'll forget it

- Set aside time during your week when you plan your romance. Use the technology that you have available to help you execute what you've planned. Don't leave it to chance

- Lay all of your plans before the Lord in prayer. He will make your plans succeed

Becoming Intimate Life-Builders

1. Using what you have learned of your spouse in the University of Us and/or their Love Language, write out a few things that you can intentionally do to bless them

2. Using what technology or organizational tools you have available, schedule dates and times to execute

3. Using the resources that you currently have or finding free ones, look for ways that you can bless them daily. Schedule a time to get fresh ideas and for implementation. Remember it's about completion, not perfection. Don't procrastinate

4. Gently give feedback for their effort if their attempt doesn't go well. Encourage the efforts made

5. Plan times for sexual intimacy, date nights, birthdays, anniversaries, vacations, etc.

For Reflection:

- Based on what you learned in the University of Us what would be the first thing to bless your spouse with? What would be the second?

Chapter 14

Rehab

If you broke your arm from a hard fall, would you cut it off and give up on it? If you had an eye infection that wasn't permanently damaging, would you ask a doctor to separate your eye from your body? I know these questions seem ridiculous, but this is what it sounds like when a husband or wife wants to separate from a wounded spouse.

Ephesians 5:31 (NLT): As the Scriptures say, "A man leaves his father and mother and is joined to his wife, and the two are united into one."

Your body parts need one another. We all get this, right? If your arm is broken, you go to a doctor to get it repaired. They put it in a cast and you wait for it to heal. During the healing process, your other arm will carry the bulk of the load. You'll accept this because you hope that your wounded arm will recover. You'll make it work for the time being because you don't want to discard the wounded arm because you know you'll need it! It's a part of who you are, and you're willing to give it time to get better. You're willing to go to rehab because it's about self-preservation.

There will be moments in your marriage when your spouse is like that wounded arm. They may be that infected eye. They are going through a difficult season and they need rehabilitation in an area where they are struggling to produce healthy results.

Don't cut them off in their injured state. After all, they are one with you! If you've experienced injuries in your physical body or a moment of sickness, then you get this. You don't go around cutting off body parts in their moments of weakness. Instead, you nourish yourself back to health.

Ephesians 5:28–29 (NLT): 28 In the same way, husbands ought to love their wives as they love their own bodies. For a man who loves his wife actually shows love for himself. 29 No one hates his own body but feeds and cares for it, just as Christ cares for the church.

Paul encourages men to lead with love. Treat our wives as our own bodies. We feed and care for our bodies. We give ourselves the essentials to grow. Your wife needs security and safety. She needs to know that she's number one in your life.

Do you love her more than your favorite sports team? Can you accept her as she is? Is she confident that she need not compete with porn or magazine models to get your attention? She needs to know that she has access to your undivided attention when she's talking to you.

She is one with you. If you had an itch on your body, you'd scratch it. When you're thirsty, you get a drink. Get hungry, and you go get something to eat. Should an injury occur, you'd seek healing.

Your wife may go through a moment when she's struggling with her identity. This may be a season that she's never encountered before in her life. She could be experiencing grief in her life. This may be a moment of promotion on the job! When she's going through life transitions, so are you. Verse 28 says we must "show love" for ourselves by showing love to her.

Paul goes even further by clarifying the kind of love we should offer our wives. It's the same love that Christ displayed on the cross for sinners. Sacrificial love is what every husband must be willing to show his wife.

You can do this, brother (in my Hulk Hogan voice)! You may

say, "Sean, you don't know my wife." Well, maybe not, but I know the power of God. I know that love conquers hate. Love can even cover sin. In fact, I am one of those imperfect people that Jesus came to save. He's changed me through his life-changing love.

Love isn't a feeling. It's a way of committing care to a person no matter what they do or have done. Love is an uncompromising commitment to give all you are to the people you care for. Love isn't contingent on the person it's being shown to. It originates within a man from God himself. Scripture teaches us that God is love, and that God lives in us. This is why love isn't predicated on the recipient. They aren't the source of what you're offering them. God is your unlimited supply.

There's a reservoir of love within you to share with your wife. You can be a healer of her hurts. Offer rehabilitation where she's wounded. When she falls you can help her to get back up again. In the same manner, you'd restore your wounded body by restoring your wife. Cover her and supply the nourishment she needs.

Till Death Do Us Part

My wife and I declared over our marriage "divorce is not an option." We're in this covenant till death do us part. This kind of determination mixed with the teachings of this book will lead to marital success. You ought to say that out loud a few times: "Divorce is not an option!"

If you've ever been through physical rehabilitation, you understand that it can get intense, and it requires patience. Your marriage may have suffered financial loss. It takes time to get things back on track. You must walk in patience with your diligence.

Please don't forget this; take baby steps. Day by day and step by step you'll rehabilitate the wounded areas of your marriage. Rehab can get frustrating because you know how the body part should work in your mind. Yet it's a struggle to move it as it should move in reality. When you see a picture of what your marriage should be in your mind that clashes with what it is in reality, it can get disheartening. Say it with me, "Divorce is not an option." I thank God that my wife and I didn't give up in our dark days. Now that we are healed from our wounded ways, we're experiencing brighter days.

Are there extreme cases when divorce should be considered? In the cases of adultery, abuse or abandonment, I'd say get wise counseling. Jesus clarified that divorce is permissible with adultery. Paul explained that if a spouse abandons their partner, they are released from their marital responsibilities. Marriage isn't signing up to be murdered, so we throw physical abuse in there as well.

All I'm saying is that sometimes things aren't as extreme as they seem. People want divorce over so-called "irreconcilable differences." In our case, we fought through it, and I hope you do, too. Can you find it in you to love one another to health?

Chapter Summary

- There will be moments in your marriage when your spouse is wounded. Though it's a difficult season they will need rehabilitation in an area where they are struggling to produce healthy results. Don't cut them off in their injured state. You are one- nourish yourself back to health

- Love isn't a feeling, It's a way of committing care to a person no matter what they do or have done. It's an uncompromising commitment to give all you are to the people you care for and it's not contingent on the person it's being shown to

- Your spouse isn't the source of what you're offering them. God is your unlimited supply

- Rehab can get frustrating but take baby steps day by day. Divorce is not an option

Becoming Intimate Life–Builders

1. Take the faults that you find in your spouse and turn them into prayer requests for their healing

2. Rely and depend on God to strengthen you through the frustration and release your disappointment to Him. Tap into His unlimited supply

3. Follow His guidance on how you can love your spouse to health

For Reflection:

- In what ways do you or your spouse appear injured? Ask God about their healing process and what you can do to gently help

Chapter 15

Space For Grace

In order for your team to succeed, you need constant unity. Any unforgiveness, untended wounds and inner resentment must be healed. When you harbor hurt, it's hard to get healed. If you aren't healed, then part of your marriage isn't growing.

You and I aren't perfect. We all need forgiveness and grace. Even though we know this for a fact, we still hold our spouses to a standard of perfection. Our expectations of their performance are set high. So when our intimate life-builder fails to execute the blueprints as designed, we take it personally.

Jesus gives a great short story about forgiveness and grace that we all must apply to our marriages. I pray that you consider yourself as you read through this parable.

Matthew 18:21–35 (NLT): 21 Then Peter came to him and asked, "Lord, how often should I forgive someone who sins against me? Seven times?" 22 "No, not seven times," Jesus replied, "but seventy times seven!

23 "Therefore, the Kingdom of Heaven can be compared to a king who decided to bring his accounts up to date with servants who had borrowed money from him. 24 In the process, one of his debtors was brought in who owed him millions of dollars. 25 He couldn't pay, so his master ordered that he be sold—along with his wife, his children, and everything he owned—to pay the debt.

26 "But the man fell down before his master and begged him, 'Please, be patient with me, and I will pay it all.' 27 Then his master was filled with pity for him, and he released him and forgave his debt.

"But when the man left the king, he went to a fellow servant who owed him a few thousand dollars. He grabbed him by the throat and demanded instant payment. "His fellow servant fell down before him and begged for a little more time. 'Be patient with me, and I will pay it,' he pleaded. 30 But his creditor wouldn't wait. He had the man arrested and put in prison until the debt could be paid in full.

31 "When some of the other servants saw this, they were very upset. They went to the king and told him everything that had happened. 32 Then the king called in the man he had forgiven and said, 'You evil servant! I forgave you that tremendous debt because you pleaded with me. 33 Shouldn't you have mercy on your fellow servant, just as I had mercy on you?' 34 Then the angry king sent the man to prison to be tortured until he had paid his entire debt. 35 "That's what my heavenly Father will do to you if you refuse to forgive your brothers and sisters from your heart."

This parable is amazing. God has forgiven the debt of our sin. After all the grace and mercy he's poured out on us, we have no right to withhold grace to those who "owe us." When someone has offended us in any way we must forgive. Make a choice to repel the hurt and release the offense.

The word forgive in the Greek language spoken during the Bible days is aphiemi. It means to absolve from payment. It means to acquit or to leave unpunished. That's what God has done for us, and that's what he will empower us to do towards others.

If your spouse has a debt you want them to repay in any way, let it go. According to Jesus' choice of words, to forgive them is to aphiemi, or absolve from payment. Let whatever they've done wrong go unpunished.

Before you say it's not fair, please consider Jesus on the cross being crucified for our crimes. He did this for sinners. Humans deserved to pay for their crimes against God. The penalty for sin was separation from God . . . death. But Jesus came so we might go unpunished and receive life in abundance!

You and I didn't deserve this release from prison. As the parable illustrates, he had mercy and extended grace. Verse 35 says we can "refuse" to forgive our brothers and sisters. When we refuse to release their offenses, we end up in a prison of pain.

The Power to Forgive

The power to forgive comes from a gratitude of being released. Do you have a grateful heart for a gracious God? God loved you before you were his child and he still loves you, even though you aren't perfect right now.

It's out of this appreciation that you refuse to place others in the same prison that Christ released you from. You have a choice to be like Jesus; a choice to release and facilitate peace.

When the disciples asked Jesus how many times a person should forgive an offender in one day, Jesus replies 490. The point of the number isn't to sit there and keep count of the many sins against you. The idea is as many times as it takes.

Forgiveness helps them, but it's for you. It keeps you from falling into a trap of bitterness. It keeps you from bearing the unnecessary burden of someone's sin. Didn't Jesus already do that? Jesus carried and killed the sin of the world on Calvary's cross. He killed sin through his shed blood at Calvary! That includes your sin, and any offender. So why revive a dead thing like sin when he paid for all the sins we've committed and ever would commit? That's amazing grace!

You and I aren't designed to carry around vengeance in our hearts. It steals the life and love out of us. Your spouse needs you to walk in grace. They need your grace on their worst day. As you walk out the principles of this parable you'll experience love in abundance in your marriage.

Chapter Summary

- You need constant unity in order to succeed in marriage

- Un-forgiveness, untended wounds and inner resentment must be healed. If not, then part of your marriage isn't growing

- When our intimate life-builder fails to execute for us we tend to take it personally

- Make a choice to repel the hurt and release the offense especially if you feel that your spouse has a debt that you want them to repay you

- The power to forgive comes from a gratitude of being released.

- Forgive as many times as it takes, it keeps you from falling into a trap of bitterness

Becoming Intimate Life-Builders

1. Make a list of the debts that you feel your spouse owes you and forgive each one by one

2. Remove the high expectations that you have of your spouse. Change your perspective from being performance driven to one of being full of grace towards them.

For Reflection:

- Take some time to reflect on what the blood of Jesus and His death accomplished for you personally. Remind yourself of what you've been forgiven of. This should serve as the foundation of your gratitude and joy that should flow to your spouse in times when you need to forgive them

Chapter 16

In-to-me-see

In the great game of baseball, a shutout is an awesome accomplishment. For those who may not know what a shutout is, it's simple. Just keep the opposing team scoreless for nine innings of baseball. As long as you've scored a point and they can't, you win the game by performing a shutout. The goal of a shutout is simple; keep the opposition from earning a single point.

Sadly, there are many husbands and wives who are striving to earn a shutout against their opposition. (I mean their spouse.) A shutout in marriage is never a winner. What does a shutout look like in your marriage?

It looks like a husband or wife stonewalling their mate. When they've decided that they'll refuse to engage in productive, loving, and intimate conversations. A person has decided to win a point by proving that they can outlast their enemy.

This isn't a good idea, but I've been guilty of this crime against my spouse plenty of times. Maybe she offended me by not responding verbally in a way that I felt honored me. It's possible that she rejected an advance for sex. She's shut me out at times as well, when she's tired of asking me to help around the house.

At that moment, what did we do? We beat the opposition by withholding kindness, gentleness, and love. It's a conscious decision to shut them out of our thoughts and put them out of the intimacy zone. They are now our opposition. They're on the other team, and we must win at all cost.

It's not about unity or intimacy anymore. We are definitely roommates at this point. It's about winning no matter what. As long as I get the win and she loses in that moment, I consider myself a winner. But when my spouse goes down, so do I. The house is divided, and we both end up wounded. It's never healthy to stonewall your spouse.

Sometimes this is a problem of wanting to control the outcome through outlasting the enemy. Possibly we may seek vengeance for something we've considered a rejection, a breach of trust or disrespect.

Your deal breakers may differ from mine. All of us must examine our hearts and discover what our buttons are. What sends you into "shutout mode"? Is it when you ask him to help you with chores and he never helps? Maybe it's when you suffer long droughts without sexual fulfillment. It may be their lack of follow through on an action plan. Is your deal breaker their silence when you're trying to understand what's on their mind? Whatever your button may be, it's important that you find it. If you don't, this will always be an entryway for division in your marriage.

I remember times when I'd be so upset I'd sit on the couch and bounce my leg as fast and hard as I could, trying to display my disdain for something she'd done. The worst part about my immature behavior is that she didn't even know why. But regardless, I wanted her to pay! Pay for what? Most times, it was something so stupid, and to make matters worse, it was something she didn't even know. I'd sleep on the edge of the bed, just to show her I didn't want to touch her. Next thing you know, I hear snoring. That would make me even angrier. Then I'd go to bed angry. This, my friends, is one of my biggest mistakes. Here's why:

Ephesians 4:26–27 (NKJV): 26 "Be angry, and do not sin": do not let the sun go down on your wrath, 27 nor give place to the devil.

I was angry and determined to defeat what I believed to be the source of my pain. So I'd shut down to win against the one who was hurting me. I repeat, most times she didn't even know why. Remember that your spouse isn't a mind reader. Let them in so you both win!

Everyone will get angry about something that happens in the house. We are emotional beings, and we will react to perceived or actual threats against us. God's word encourages us to deal with it before dark. If you hold on to the injury overnight, the anger takes root in your heart. These roots may become bitterness, envy, resentment, and retaliation.

The fruit of this may be the moment you shut out your spouse. A simple mistake from your spouse may cause an over-the-top reaction from you. But the reason you implode or explode in that moment is that it brought out fruit from a bitter root.

If you've been holding disappointment and unspoken frustrations in your heart, you'll give place to the devil. You give the devil rights of interpretation. He'll interpret your pain for you. By the time he's done interpreting their actions against you, you'll despise them and want them to pay for the crimes they've committed against you.

The crimes may be: failing to pay a bill on time; not finishing their end of the chores; not helping with the kids; failing to be romantic; refusing to have sex with you last night when you asked; leaving clothes on the floor; or not taking initiative.

These crimes committed against you become grounds for punishment. By the time the devil is done in the dark, you'll feel justified in destroying them by the day. They didn't do these things because they're out to hurt you, right? They intentionally didn't pay the bill on time to destroy you? Come on, people! Maybe they're just as human as you are. They've got areas where they need you to cover them, rather than convict them. They need grace instead of disgust.

Only to Protect Her

Believe it or not, my justification for shutting my wife out was to protect her. I wouldn't let her into my thoughts because I didn't want to express the frustrations in my head. Sometimes I feared that it would come out wrong. Other times, I thought that if I'd opened up and expressed myself, she'd get all defensive and we'd end up arguing. In my mind, I'd play out the scenarios of honesty, and they all ended up hurting her. So what did I do? I shut her out to protect her. Please understand that I really meant no harm to her. But in my mind, I saw talking it out as a lose-lose situation.

The problem with this thinking is that it gives me no outlet, and her no inlet. I'm holding in what should be talked out. This behavior is unfair to her and it's destructive to me. Unfair to her because she can't offer justification about my unspoken frustrations. It's destructive to me because in my mind I've decided that she did it to hurt me. So I'm growing angrier and angrier by the minute over a misinterpretation of her intentions.

Can you remember moments in your relationship like this? You ever pitched a shutout? Here's a suggestion . . . realize that stalemates are destructive. Displaying a hardened heart towards your spouse will never bring you the resolve you want. If you shut them out, you simultaneously trap your pain within. I repeat, if you shut them out, you simultaneously trap the pain within. This is a wrecking ball to your home. Eventually, intimacy is gone and the home will collapse.

I encourage you to refuse to accuse. One way that I've conquered anger was to release the offense. The moment I feel that my wife is my enemy, I know that that's a problem within me. Please hear me out: there are moments when your life is in danger with a physically abusive spouse; drug abuse around you or your child; a spouse has abandoned the relationship; or a spouse is sleeping with another person. These are serious offenses, and in these extreme cases, a separation for healing is in order. Sometimes, divorce is in order.

But mostly, people are offended over money fights, uncompleted chores, dropping the ball in daily tasks, and unmet expectations. These aren't grounds for divorce, but they can become gateways to division. It's a heart problem here. You have the power to release the offense by dropping the accusation.

Let me put it this way: release the accusation, and then have the conversation. When you release the accusation and then have the conversation, you seek to see it from their side and explain how it affected you. This is productive, and should be done the day of the conflict.

Sleeping in other rooms, ignoring your spouse, giving short answers or snappy remarks are a sure sign you're in shutout mode. There are many other signs, but you get the point. Love wins when the shutout ends. Ask the Lord to strengthen you to overcome the anxiety, stress, and fear of healthy conversation. I didn't say confrontation, but healthy conversation.

In trying to protect my wife from a confrontation, I robbed her of healthy conversation. There was a time when I saw her as my enemy, instead of my best friend. This put me in the perspective of conquering her instead of comforting her. What a waste of time and energy!

If you're in the position of holding it in or stalemating your mate, please understand that you're in a prison of pain. Set an appointment and try to have a healthy conversation.

That last thing I'll say here is this. You can't control their reaction, but you can control yours. When you set up a time to talk and approach your spouse to talk it out, do it in love. If they don't react in a manner you wish, it's okay.

You don't always react well to God's loving conversations and advice, do you? You have moments when you fail to respond to God's direction and correction. So, you're not perfect. Neither is your spouse. There has to be an abundance of grace when you sit across from them to get out what's on your heart. But let them into your world, into your heart, and that's the pathway to intimacy.

Chapter Summary

- A shutout in marriage is never a winner. When you argue with your spouse, although one of you may win the argument- you've both lost

- Identifying your personal deal breakers will help prevent entryways of division in your marriage

- God encourages us to deal with our anger before dark so that roots of bitterness, envy, resentment and retaliation don't take

- When we hold on to disappointment and unspoken frustration in our hearts, we give place to the devil and his interpretation of our pain

- Displaying a hardened heart towards your spouse will never bring you the resolve you want. Shutting them out simultaneously traps your pain within you

Becoming Intimate Life-Builders

1. Set an appointment to try to have a healthy conversation

2. Identify the ways you've experienced rejection, frustration and disappointment with your spouse and prayerfully discuss it

3. Identify the areas that your heart has hardened towards your spouse and prayerfully discuss to bring healing to your marriage

For Reflection:

- What are the accusations that you have believed and are holding against your spouse? Ask God to show you the truth about your spouse in those areas to help you drop the accusation and walk in forgiveness

Chapter 17

Tame The Tongue

Have you ever said something you regret? We've said many things to each other that we wish we could take back. Speaking out of emotion and the heat of the moment has been an intimacy killer in our home. We've had to learn the art of taming the tongue.

You could say that "competitor" is my middle name. I hate to lose, and don't mind a great debate. When I married my wife, she was somewhat introverted. I would become so frustrated when she didn't agree with me or see things my way. So you know what I'd do? I'd switch into debate mode and try to win the battle of being right by arguing her down. I'd say hurtful things and bring up past mistakes of hers to validate my argument and win the fight.

Bluntly stated, I was foolish, chauvinistic, and prideful. I was not thinking clearly because I hadn't paused to process the real problems. I shifted from being a loving spouse to prosecuting attorney, trying to win the case for my perspective and in the process, destroying a person. My tongue became a tool of trouble.

A few years into our marriage, my wife and I came into agreement to calm these "intense fellowships." If God doesn't yell at us, we won't yell at one another. No one is a child to be babysat in our marriage. So, we mutually agreed that hollering at one another is beneath us and immature. Just like that, we stopped yelling at one another. We decided to respect and honor each other. Will you commit to guarding your mouth from killing your spouse? Will you tame your tongue?

Picture this; words are like containers. Let's take a cup, for example. You can fill it with purified water or poison. If we were to take a sample of what your words are filled with towards your spouse, would we discover that they were poisonous or prosperous?

Proverbs 10:11 (NLT): The words of the godly are a life-giving fountain; the words of the wicked conceal violent intentions.

Your words can be a life-giving fountain or violent and destructive. In that verse it says that the wicked person's words are filled with violent intentions. When I think of the word wicked, I picture the twisted wick of a candle. Twisted intentions may be at the root of our destructive fruit.

When I was being controlling and faultfinding, my heart was in the wrong place. I wanted to force her to change from her opinions and ways of seeing to mine. As if I'm perfect and all wise . . . as if her personality and opinion was inferior to mine. That's a twisted perspective!

My words were the fruit of a corrupt root. My need to control her came from bondages in my own heart. The need to control her to secure my own happiness and security was at the heart of all the confrontation. What's at the root of your words?

Might I suggest that you write before you recite? Before you say the next thing, before you engage in a war of words, pause and put your thoughts on paper. Pray to your Heavenly Father and ask him to show you why you feel how you do.

A question you can ask yourself is this: why do I feel like control is being stripped away from me? If you blame your spouse, that's the wrong answer. Your source of security, power, and peace is God. If ever you feel that your power, peace, or security is being stripped away, go to God in prayer. Bring a pencil and paper with you. Allow the Lord to speak to you and reveal what's going on in your heart.

Writing what you think is at the root of the fruit can tame your tongue. You might even want to write out what you need to say to your spouse. Be careful to drop anything that may be an accusation, insult, or sarcasm. Make sure that your words are filtered through love, grace, and mercy. Write it before you recite it.

Proverbs 10:13 (NLT): Wise words come from the lips of people with understanding, but those lacking sense will be beaten with a rod.

Please don't miss the wisdom in that verse. Your words, when filtered through understanding, will bring healing to the situation. That's what we want, right? We want the conflict resolved and problems solved. Those lacking sense will continue to experience pain or be beaten with a rod. I was that guy being beaten with a rod for years.

Roommates don't need intimacy. But even roommates want understanding. It's a heartbreaking thing when spouses are out for blood against one another and can't agree. You're not just roommates, you're intimate life-builders. Get rid of home-dividing, intimacy-killing, and destructive behaviors!

Simple Solutions

Meet with your spouse to speak your heart. I've suggested this to many couples, and it's a game changer. A simple appointment would be scheduled to set a time to talk. This can skyrocket your communication in the right direction. We like to call them appointments. Instead of discussing serious topics when the other person isn't ready, give them a heads-up. Let them know that there's something on your heart that needs to be dealt with before dark.

Setting an appointment gives you time to pray and gather what you need to say in a loving way. It also gives your spouse time to get ready to hear you and offer their undivided attention.

Understand that this isn't a time to accuse, it's an attempt to share what's on your heart or to get clarity. It may be a time to change a plan or discuss why you strayed from the path.

Please note that this works if both parties give each other an opportunity to speak their minds without retaliation. This isn't about fighting, but uniting. This isn't a court, and no one is on trial. Listen to what the other person says and is saying. Leave sarcasm and insults out of the conversation.

Proverbs 10:32 (NLT): The lips of the godly speak helpful words, but the mouth of the wicked speaks perverse words.

Sometimes sarcasm is a way to take a shot at someone under the umbrella of comedy. But many times it's a way to insult the person you're speaking with and cause injury. Let your words be helpful to the situation. If you guard your mouth from killing your spouse, you bring healing to the house.

Who doesn't want a peaceful house? I can assure you of this; you must fight for unity in your home. It isn't automatic, and it doesn't just happen. It takes work from both the husband and the wife.

Healing in the House

Proverbs 12:18 (NLT): Some people make cutting remarks, but the words of the wise bring healing.

Bring healing to your home by cutting out the cutting remarks. There's no room for harmful words. Cutting remarks may include bringing up their past mistakes again. These remarks may be destructive criticism or complaining.

In each relationship, the utensils that cut are different. The utensils that cut are the words that offend your best friend. Why destroy your own home? It makes no sense. The energy used to destroy your home with hurtful words could be substituted with words that heal. Can you find words that encourage or affirm? Use positive and life-giving words with the same energy from your mouth.

Proverbs 21:9 (HCSB): Better to live on the corner of a roof than to share a house with a nagging wife.

This verse clarifies how being in a home with a nagging person, whether it's the wife or husband, makes the other person wish they were somewhere else. The person wants to escape to a life on the roof to get away from their spouse.

Proverbs 21:19 (HCSB): Better to live in a wilderness than with a nagging and hot-tempered wife.

When a spouse is angry and spewing insults, the other person would rather be homeless than to stay in an abusive and hostile atmosphere. What's the point here?

If you tame your tongue you can heal the home. Your words flow from out of your spirit, through your mind, and out your mouth. This is a beautiful picture if your mind is under the counsel of the Holy Spirit. God speaks life to your spirit, and it flows through your mouth and heals the home.

To My Sisters

My sister, will you allow the Holy Spirit to rule your tongue? Even though you may be frustrated with your spouse, or fed up with the lack of help around the house, allow God to give peace to your soul. You'll speak what the Lord gives you and in doing so, you'll heal your house.

One thing that your husband needs is honor. There will be little intimacy where a man's disrespected. If your husband is being confronted, criticized, or challenged by you he's bound to implode or explode. Either way, you won't get the results you want through the madness of your mouth. But you can bring healing to him with the ministry of your mouth. Consider this verse of wisdom:

Proverbs 27:15 (HCSB): An endless dripping on a rainy day and a nagging wife are alike.

Our home has a master bathroom attached to my bedroom. After a shower I laid down, trying to get rest, but the shower head was dripping heavy drops of water. I thought I could ignore them at first, but then they became an irritating distraction. It was an endless, irritating, dripping faucet.

A husband knows when there's a problem, but he may process it in a different manner than you would prefer. To nag and complain at him as if he's a child is a bad move. It will backfire every time. Ask the Holy Spirit what to say. Set an appointment, and be patient.

To My Brothers

Proverbs 13:3 (NLT): Those who control their tongue will have a long life; opening your mouth can ruin everything.

Cursing, confrontation, criticism, and clocking out will get you nothing but trouble. Control your tongue and give long life to your marriage. There are moments when you should share your thoughts. But sometimes you're upset and you need a time out. Take your time out before you say something you'll regret.

Your wife can be your best friend, but she's not your best man. It's wrong for us to treat our wife as one of the guys. Cursing, confronting, and criticizing looks are actions more like in a locker room than a bedroom. If you don't want to destroy your marriage, I encourage you to control your tongue. Love should guide the words that come out of your mouth. If you want to graduate from roommate to intimate lover, you've got to tame the tongue.

Proverbs 18:21 (NLT): The tongue can bring death or life; those who love to talk will reap the consequences.

God's word is clear here. Our words can bring life to the home. My wife and I fought back from the brink of divorce by adopting healthy habits. One of the main areas we developed was the tongue. I had to tame my tongue from reaping destructive consequences.

Proverbs 26:21 (NLT): A quarrelsome person starts fights as easily as hot embers light charcoal or fire lights wood.

Brothers, if we refuse to instigate arguments with cutting remarks, the fire will die down. If we love our spouse the same way that Christ loves us, we can avoid burning the house down. When we engage in an argument or continue in confrontation, we add fuel to the fire.

Give your wife the same grace that God has given you. Be gentle towards your bride, even when she may be out of line. There's a reservoir of grace inside of you. The same forgiveness that Christ has extended to you, you can extend to her. Let this mind-set govern your conversations and bring life and love to your marriage.

A Final Thought on Taming the Tongue

It's easy to find fault in our mate. None of us are perfect. We all make mistakes in areas that need improvement. Anyone can complain and criticize. My encouragement to you is to find something positive to say. A few suggestions:

- Compliment your mate instead of giving complaints.

- Confess your mistakes instead of expressing strong disapproval of theirs.

- Encourage constructively instead of criticizing destructively.

Taming the tongue is not just about what you should stop saying, but what you should say. You have the power to bring life, love, and healing if you choose to do so.

Chapter Summary

- Speaking out of emotion and the heat of the moment is an intimacy killer

- Your words can be a life-giving fountain or violent and destructive

- Drop anything that may be an accusation, insult or sarcasm

- Your words when filtered through understanding, will bring healing to the situation

- Meet with your spouse to speak your heart by setting an appointment. This is your opportunity to speak your mind without retaliation

Becoming Intimate Life-Builders

1. If you yell at your spouse for any reason- immediately stop

2. Stop the practice of speaking out of emotion and in the heat of the moment

3. Try writing what you need to express to your spouse before speaking to them

4. Drop all accusations, insults and sarcasm

5. Schedule a time to speak with them to share what's on your heart and gain clarity

6. Give each other an opportunity to speak without seeking retaliation

For Reflection:

- What kind of encouraging and life-giving confessions has God given you regarding your mate? How can you use them when constructively encouraging your mate?

Chapter 18

Indecent Exposure

Above all, put on love--the perfect bond of unity.

Colossians 3:14 (HCSB)

Two separate items must be held together by something. A binding agent is necessary. Paul teaches the Church that the perfect binding agent is love. What binds a home together?

Beyond all of the financial wisdom, parenting strategies, or cleaning preferences is the virtue of love. Above being right or having all the perfect answers in your marriage is walking in unconditional love towards your spouse.

In verse 14 it says to put on love. It's like we are given a choice to wake up and put on clothes or to leave the house exposed. If a person were to leave the house naked, they'd be arrested for indecent exposure. Many of us are guilty of indecent exposure to our spouse!

If we engage in conversation, sex, parenting, or any other activity outside of the binding agent of love, we fall into an incomplete bond. Another way of seeing this is that it is an immature bond. You don't know how many times I've given the right answer the wrong way. Truth should be spoken in love. Being right just for the sake of proving your spouse wrong destroys the bond. What good is it to be critical and right about a point of discussion if you destroy a person in the process?

Sex should be enjoyable. I mentioned sex in this chapter because it's important that we engage in passionate sex. The core of a healthy sex life is love.

You and your spouse should maintain a healthy sex life. You should discuss what that looks like for you. But I want to give a little advice here. Sex outside of love is lust expressed through a physical act. Sex fueled by love is a reaffirmation of your covenant.

Allow the bedroom to become a place to express your unconditional love for each other. It should be pleasurable and purposeful. Before engaging in sex, remember the why behind the what. Get your mind right by putting on love, the perfect bond of unity. What better way for couples to express their oneness than sex? Two physically become one body.

If your bodies are moving, but the person doesn't move your heart, it's an incomplete gesture and lacks fulfillment. It doesn't support the unity. Listen; you and your spouse are married. God has blessed your bed! Make use of this God-given freedom.

I'd encourage couples to exclude pornography from your covenant. If you need to see manufactured actors or sometimes victims of human trafficking prostituted on a screen to spice up your sex life, then something is wrong. This means that the source of the fire in your bedroom is looking at and lusting after someone else's physical portrayal of sexual bliss. Your sex life is based on a lie instead of love. What a cheap substitute! You can achieve sexual fulfillment and satisfying sexual intimacy. But it begins with love.

Do a heart check . . . has lust taken the place of love? If so, you must graduate from being led by your flesh to being led by love. The beautiful thing about love is that it can be put on at will. You can choose to adorn yourself with unconditional love. That means you can, at will, love your spouse with their flaws and all. The reservoir we can draw from is God, for he is love. There's an unending supply of love we can put on through prayer and surrender to the voice of God.

Tips for Sexual Intimacy

Sex is one of those awkward and taboo subjects for people. But you can't get four chapters into the Bible before sex is mentioned. When God made man, he said we were good. He created sex for enjoyment and procreation. So sex within marriage is good. Can I get an amen! There are great resources on sexual intimacy that I'd suggest you read: The Keys to Sexual Fulfillment in Marriage by Jimmy Evans and Sacred Sex by Tony Evans.

I suggest that you and your spouse set an appointment to discuss your likes and dislikes for your bedroom. Sexual fulfillment is about love, passion, and pleasure. You should seek to serve and be served. Ask questions, discover needs, and try to meet those needs. Discover your marriage's sexual identity. There's no one way that fits all. Neither is it wise to bring preferences from previous relationships as imposed demands on your spouse. Start the sex talk!

I can't stress this point enough: your spouse isn't a mind reader. They don't "just know" how you want it. Sometimes they don't know how often you want it. These conversations don't make sex any less romantic or spontaneous. It will lead to greater fulfillment and needs met. Have a fun sex talk! It need not be all deep and stressful. It's okay to laugh and have fun with these discussions.

Another reason you should have this conversation is that it removes the guesswork. It gives options for variety, and a break from the monotony of the same routine. Your focus will be less on disappointment or anxiety and more on the devotion.

There are many people who are insecure about their self-image. They look down on themselves and prefer to have sex in the dark, or they shun lingerie. But if your spouse is turned on by what they see, you may be killing the intimacy. You see, unconditional love is a unifier. Love can bring healing, even in the bedroom.

For most women, sexual intimacy begins in the morning, with her mind. Begin with a compliment or a bouquet sent. It might begin with a simple text with a special message throughout the day. Getting your wife in the mood doesn't always require a new diamond ring. (Though I'm sure she wouldn't mind one.)

Many of us guys go for the home run, but our wives would be happy if we'd become consistent base hitters. She may need a foot massage, with no intention of sex afterwards. She may need you to look her in the eyes as she shares with you the details of her day.

This kind of thinking and action requires you to put on love. Love removes us from selfish or self-centered thinking. Romance is about pleasing the other person and doing something special. What's the reward? Well, you may not get one at once. That's the love part. It's not like you pay the fee of a kind gesture for intense sex. You set an atmosphere in her heart that turns a spark to a flame. You can show through consistent action that she's most important to you.

What can you do today to show her what you said to her? What special things can you do throughout the day to show your love for her? You will put on your love and then Google! That's right, Google romantic ideas or special things you can do on a budget.

Now, ladies, I must caution you. When your husband tries and attempts to make your day, be careful not to be critical of his care. It's very important to recognize when a man is trying to step it up. Don't shoot the man down because he didn't meet your highest expectation.

See his heart behind the action before you give a negative reaction. The worst thing you can do is give him no reaction at all when he's trying to be romantic. Pick the right time and place to give helpful hints and constructive criticism. But when he shows up with flowers that are the wrong color for the occasion, give him grace. Get the message behind the action before you give a negative reaction.

Show Men Some Skin

Most men want to see some skin! Men are visually stimulated. What you wear around the house matters. If you're always conservative or revealing nothing appealing to the eye, you're doing yourself a disservice. Help a brother out and bring sexy back. One of your greatest gifts is your attire. You can be Christian and sexy. Married for years and still attracted to each other. He wants to see you sexy even while you clean. At one marriage conference women discovered from our men that they love a woman in jogging pants and t-shirt. I'm sure your man would love to fill you in on what turns him on. In the bedroom, hook that brother up with that lingerie!

I'm not saying you've got to get all dolled up all day long, but your husband married a beautiful woman that he'd like to see. Give him the eye candy. Show him that body, even when you're not in front of anyone else or going out somewhere special.

IPC

There's something my wife, and I coined as a phrase to describe what most men we surveyed want . . . Intense Physical Contact, or IPC. Most women want romance, but most men want IPC.

In most cases, a man need not be romanced throughout the day to prepare him for a sexual encounter. Flip on the lights and put on something nice and he's ready to go! Now I may exaggerate here, but I know you've got this one. He wants you to communicate your affection for him through intense physical contact. At the University of Us, you found out how he likes things to be done. Well, put actions behind that degree.

Let's face it; we're all busy. Everyone's time crunched. My wife and I have three teenagers in school, with sports and all that comes with raising them. We pastor a church, make music, write books, mentor people, and clean the house. We still make time for romance and IPC.

She and I were together before the children, the church, and all the other commitments. It's not right to adopt all of these responsibilities and place those things as first priority. Your spouse comes first, after God. He's worth planning the IPC. She's worth putting on love and fighting to keep the perfect bond.

If you want a long-lasting marriage, avoid indecent exposure. Cover your good advice and your bedroom with love. Everything you do can be done in love. It'll strengthen your bond more than you know.

Did you put your love on today?

Chapter Summary

- Beyond all of the financial wisdom, parenting strategies, or cleaning preferences is the virtue of love

- What good is it to be critical and right about a point of discussion if you destroy your spouse in the process? Truth should be spoken in love

- Love can be put on at will, choose to adorn yourself with unconditional love.

- The reservoir we draw from is God, for He is love

- Discover your marriage's sexual identity. Remember, your spouse isn't a mind reader

- Romance is about pleasing the other person and doing something special

Becoming Intimate Life–Builders

1. Regarding your spouse, adorn yourself with unconditional love

2. Discuss with your spouse what a healthy sex life looks like for you. Take the time to discover your marriage's sexual identity

3. Husbands- Create consistency by planning non sexual and romantic encounters for her to display her importance to you

4. Wives- Be prepared for spontaneous encounters. Be willing to show some skin as men are visually stimulated. He most likely will not need to be romanced but he will need IPC

For Reflection:

- Assess the sexual health of your marriage. In what ways can you serve your spouse better?

Chapter 19

Date Your Mate

I don't know what your schedule looks like on a daily basis. Some people have very flexible schedules, while others are working overtime like crazy. Many people reading this have large families, while others are empty nesters. You may be married and still in college or living the retired life. Whatever place you find yourself in I want to encourage you to date your mate.

What I mean by date your mate is simple. Find a time you all carve out for yourselves to get away from the kids, bills, the house, and the everyday routine. A date is an appointed time with your spouse when you enjoy one another's company. Time to do something special together.

It may be something fun, like taking dance lessons. It may be romantic, like a picnic at the park. Can you try a new restaurant in a different part of town? It may even be a romantic dinner for two at your candlelit dining room table. A date is a designated time to keep the fire burning in your relationship.

Thank God for our children and places of work, but you need a break from them. Create moments exclusively set aside for each other. If you assess the hours you put into work, parenting, church, or hobbies, you may discover that you spend little intimate time alone together. So again I encourage you to date your mate. Set a time or a day during the week that's reserved for your best friend.

If you have a date night, what can you do to spice it up? My wife and I set up our date nights, and for the most part we've kept them. Sometimes we've fallen off track. Most of those "off track" times were when we were on borderline burnout. Some of you are long overdue for a date night makeover.

Date Night Makeover

Maybe you're on a budget right now and have little to spend towards what you think to be an amazing date night. But I'd like to encourage you to look up things you can do in your city for free! You'll be amazed at the articles out there that you'll find if you make the time to search it out. There's no excuse for a lack of intimate time with your spouse. You both deserve it, and your marriage future depends on it.

Some of you don't like to try anything new. That's okay, if that's what your spouse has agreed to. I'm merely suggesting to think outside of the box when you're on a budget. It shouldn't require a birthday for candles and cards. It shouldn't take a national holiday to get you two out of the house. Do something special with your special one.

I'd like to challenge you to find points of discussion. What I mean by this is that before the date, prepare for the conversation. Why? Because it helps to break the routine of the same old questions and answers. There's a lot of real estate to be explored in their hearts and minds. When you ask fresh and unique questions it can lead the conversation to introspective answers.

Find a trusted babysitter and give yourselves a much-needed break. Focus on your number one priority. Priorities are communicated and demonstrated by time. If we took inventory of where you invest your time, how much have you committed to dating your mate?

If you feel that it's impossible, I'll submit to you that nothing is impossible. Turn off your favorite show to spend quality time with your favorite person. Date in the morning or catch a lunch together. Put effort into it. Carve out the time by saying no to lesser priorities. I can't put into words how valuable quality time has been for my wife and me. It's definitely a game changer.

I've seen husbands devote themselves to their jobs, logging hours above and beyond the call of duty. But when it came time for their spouse, they pushed her to the side. To make matters worse, they expect her to accept a marriage void of intimacy. People need more than your verbal affirmation; they need a physical demonstration. If your wife or husband is your priority, how have you communicated that beyond your words?

Chapter Summary

- A date is a designated time to keep the fire burning in your relationship. Set a time or day during the week that's reserved for your best friend

- If you're on a budget and have little to spend, look up things you can do in your city for free. There's no excuse for a lack of intimate time with your spouse

- Carve out time by saying no to lesser priorities

Becoming Intimate Life-Builders

1. Set a time or a day during the week that's reserved for dating your mate

2. Look up special things that you can do in your city with your spouse according to your budget

3. Find a trusted babysitter to take care of the kids (if applicable)

4. Treat your mate with the same level of interest and excitement as you did on your first date

5. Put your full energy and effort into the date, ask questions like you're getting to know them all over again. Never grow complacent with your spouse

For Reflection:

- What creative things can you think of to make your date nights exciting and energizing for the both of you?

Chapter 20

Wanna Get Away?

My wife and I had great mentors in our lives. Bishop Kevin Dickerson and Pastor Sonjia Dickerson are like spiritual parents to us. They live an example of what a marriage is supposed to be. I'm grateful for the God in them that they allow to shine through.

I'll never forget one lesson they taught my wife and me early on in our ministry. We've been leading the Crossroads Church now for 10 years. They've been mentoring throughout this time and this lesson has stuck with us all those years.

They taught us to take a vacation once a quarter at the least. At the time they gave us that instruction, we hadn't been on a vacation since our honeymoon, which would've been seven years before that moment.

We didn't see how we could afford it. Didn't even have a babysitter at the time for our infants and toddler children. Then there was the thought of all of the work that needed to be done around the house and at work. It seemed like an impossibility.

In our minds we had every reason for why we couldn't get away. In their minds they could see why getting away was a mandate! We needed a break, but truth be told, we really couldn't see it.

Do you need to get away right now? Are you and your spouse in need of a break from the kids? Could you take a few days to get rest and relaxation? If you put your mind to it, you can do it.

Make it Happen

After my wife and I got past our excuses, we finally took a trip to San Antonio, Texas. We visited the famous Riverwalk Canal. From Fort Worth that's about a 4-hour drive. Scraping up just enough money to get a cheap hotel, we made it happen. It took everything within us to trust a babysitter with our precious children. After spending the money for the hotel and gas we had just enough to split meals at the restaurants on the Riverwalk.

It was great! I'll never forget how much we enjoyed relaxing, walking, and talking. Eating, sleeping, and we enjoyed the intimacy that all married lovers should . . . IPC! That trip changed our lives forever. Their advice has been our rule of practice after that conversation.

Lots of couples have sat in my office and listened to us give this same advice. Some have listened and applied it, while others ignored it and denied it. Which couple will you be? I hope you'll listen and receive the wisdom as my wife and I did.

You may not be able to afford the fanciest hotels or the choicest of foods. When you think of vacationing, you may have something extravagant in mind. For my wife and me, we've even taken stay-cations, just driving 30 minutes away from Fort Worth to Dallas to take a break for a night or two. The reward is that we go home rested and refreshed. Who doesn't want to get rest and be refreshed?

I was the guy who thought I didn't need it. I undervalued rest and overvalued work. Have you ever noticed what God did during creation week? On the seventh day of creation he took a rest from his labors. Why does an all-powerful God need rest? In actuality, he doesn't. He established a Sabbath day so we might learn to enjoy a day of rest. That's what the word Sabbath means, a cessation from labor.

If a Sabbath Day was important enough for God to create, then it must be essential for us to imitate. In your marriage you'll need a rest from your labors as you are building your vision. The greater the vision, the more rest required. Take a break along the way and enjoy the process of your progress.

The Principle of the Pit Stop

My wife and I attended a NASCAR racing event. You really don't get the full impact of the speed at which these cars move until you hear and see one go by you in real time. It's an amazing experience that we'll never forget.

One thing I noticed was the pit stop process. After so many laps of intense speed and wear and tear, the cars pull in for a pit stop. Their crew goes to work on replacing the worn-out tires and refilling the empty gas tanks. After the pit stop, the car gets right back into the race.

I believe that we all need to experience a pit stop! Pull over and be refilled and refreshed. This doesn't mean that you're quitting the race. It doesn't mean that those moments in the pit will cause you to quit. It's actually the opposite. If you don't pull over by choice, you'll burn out the engine and lose the race altogether.

Once you set up a shared vision, you're enrolled in the University of Us, and you're living out your values, you must get away. My wife and I will never go back to a life on burnout. We've eliminated every excuse, and we put vacations to use. I suggest you do the same. Plan a vacation as soon as possible.

One more thought on getting away. Make sure that you don't take work with you! Leave the laptop at home. Don't answer calls you know will lead to drama and distraction. We choose to stay away from social media on our vacations. If you're going to maximize your vacation time, get away from all the noise.

Give Me a Break!

Sometimes you need what we call at the Crossroads Church "me time." We all need time away from everyone. Break away from your spouse, children, extended family, and work. As married couples you don't need to do everything together. It's okay to get a break.

As I'm writing this book, my wife is on a trip with a good friend of hers. I'm watching the children for a few days so she can get away. After all, a happy wife makes a happy life. While she is away, I enjoyed me a sci-fi movie I know she would not enjoy.

About twice a year I send my wife away to get a massage. I don't like massages, but she loves them. We don't have to go together. I'm a gym rat. So I like to spend hours working out. She doesn't want to go for that long. We give each other freedom and room to breathe. For your sake, take a break.

I hope you won't force your spouse to do everything with you all the time. Remember that your interests aren't all the same. There has to be give and take. Allow your spouse to take a break without feeling guilty about it. Allow yourself to get away for a coffee break. It may be for an hour or for a few days. You may be surprised how refreshed you'll be when you get back to your family.

Chapter Summary

- Take a vacation once a quarter at the least, take a break for a night or two

- The reward is that you go home rested and refreshed

- Don't take work with you, don't answer calls and stay away from social media

- Sometimes, you need time away from everyone, you don't need to do everything as a couple, allow your spouse to take a break without feeling guilty about it

Becoming Intimate Life-Builders

1. Evaluate the Last time you took a vacation with your mate. If it's been over a year it's time to go on a vacation even if you find a local get-a-way (staycation)

2. Discuss with your mate how many vacations you want to take each year and where you would like to visit

3. Plan and execute regardless of what your budget may be

For Reflection:

- Are you overdue for a vacation? What's obstacles do you feel are stopping you from executing your vacation and how will you overcome them?

Chapter 21

Faithing Through

All I have seen teaches me to trust the Creator for all I have not seen.

~ Ralph Waldo Emerson

What do you do when your spouse isn't ready to attend the University of Us? Some people might say fake it till you make it. I completely disagree! There's no point in denying trouble in paradise. They may not be ready for a spiritual makeover. You can't force their readiness level. But there are a few things you can do by faith until they get with the program.

Pray without ceasing: I'm not talking about panicking; I'm talking about praying. God responds to our faith and trust in him. As you pray to God on their behalf, don't complain about them. Remember that you are one. Pray for them with the intensity you'd pray for yourself. Pray as the Holy Spirit guides you. A great book on prayer if you'd like to read it is The Circle Maker by Mark Batterson. When you take your needs to God in prayer, he makes sure they're supplied!

Stay in the place of grace: This is something you do by faith. It's not always easy to release the debt you think they owe you. You'll need faith in God's love for you. You'll need faith that God's love will empower you. The good news about this whole grace thing is that God has an abundant supply that he will multiply in your life.

Colossians 3:17 (NLT): 17 And whatever you do or say, do it as a representative of the Lord Jesus, giving thanks through him to God the Father.

Faith your part: you can't control their actions, but you can control your reactions. Your actions are done in faith to the Lord as worship offering. When you serve your spouse regardless of what they're doing, it's an act of obedience to God your Father.

Know that your Actions have Impact:

1 Corinthians 7:13–16 (NLT): 13 And if a Christian woman has a husband who is not a believer and he is willing to continue living with her, she must not leave him. 14 For the Christian wife brings holiness to her marriage, and the Christian husband brings holiness to his marriage. Otherwise, your children would not be holy, but now they are holy. 15 (But if the husband or wife who isn't a believer insists on leaving, let them go. In such cases the Christian husband or wife is no longer bound to the other, for God has called you to live in peace.) 16 Don't you wives realize that your husbands might be saved because of you? And don't you husbands realize that your wives might be saved because of you?

There's a bit of meat on these bones here. In this letter, Paul's giving marriage wisdom to the Church. This passage sheds light on what to do when you have a spouse that doesn't share your Christian values. I will add to that as well, that they're not living Christ-like. Do you give up on them? Should you move on with your life?

Verse 15 states that if a person has abandoned the marriage, let them go. There's a point where a person has checked out of their commitment to the cause. They've abandoned their covenant vows and aren't giving any effort to bring a resolution to the marriage institution. Paul says that you've walked by faith and kept your end of the covenant, but in light of their unwillingness to support, you can move on from the marriage.

Verses 13–14 address the lifestyle of a Christian spouse that's willing to walk by faith. You have the power to win a person to Christ through your actions. If you are walking by faith, in love and in servitude, you can win them to Christ.

16 Don't you wives realize that your husbands might be saved because of you? And don't you husbands realize that your wives might be saved because of you?

So faith it, till you make it. You can control your actions and it'll eventually impact their reactions. When they see your willingness to respect and love in spite of their mistakes, it's a lesson in grace. It's the gospel preached through your actions that'll win them t faith in Christ. You become a conduit of grace and mercy.

This is why the fake it till you make it stuff doesn't work. People can see through a phony. What a nonbeliever needs to see is why they should believe! They don't need an actor; they need to see an authentic display of the love of Christ. Are you willing to allow Christ's life to be reflected in you? If so, you may see an amazing turnaround in your marriage.

What Does This Look Like?

A few examples for men are to turn off the TV and spend quality time talking with her. Go out of your way to be romantic. Sync that calendar and find out what she likes to do. Then sacrifice time to enjoy life with her.

For women this means play the video game with him. You may not like them, but you love him. It may be allowing him to leave the house without calling him every 10 minutes to see where he is. Engaging in passionate sex instead of holding out on him may communicate this as well.

This may mean that you go solo to church and don't beat them up for not going with you. You may have to go by yourself for a while. Don't condemn them for their lack of attendance. Go to worship, then come back home and through your lifestyle, win them. Get rid of the nudges during messages while they're being preached. Eliminate "I told you so." I hope you're getting the point. They won't need to be forced to read the Bible if you live it out before them; they'll read the gospel in you.

Saved to God

When you go to work as a believer, your work environment may not reflect your Christian faith. Does this mean you abort your faithfulness to God? If you go around your unsaved loved ones or friends, is that the time to turn down your light because they walk in darkness? Of course not! You're still that city set on a hill or a candle that lights the room.

We need to light the room within the confines of our homes. For this book's purposes, we must be a light to our spouse and children. I'm not talking about being preachy or beating them over the head with Scripture. I'm referring to how you carry yourself. When we seek first the kingdom of God and his righteousness, the Lord supplies our daily needs.

Jesus lives in your heart and his Spirit abides in you. This means your joy doesn't come from an external source, including your spouse. If you allow any human to decide your level of success, then you give them a place of influence that belongs to God alone. No man should have control over your state of mind, emotions, and feelings. Through Christ you get access to peace, joy, and righteousness. Regardless of what's happening in your environment, your internal climate must be regulated by God alone. So it can be hot in the house, but cool in your spirit! It can be a hostile environment, but you're walking with peace that passes all understanding guarding your heart and mind.

This is why Scripture speaks of guarding your heart above everything. Because if you allow outside influences to determine the climate of the heart, you'll give power to your problems. Christ must be the head of your life, the ruler of your heart and your ultimate source. Jesus makes you complete because your spouse can't compete. Your spouse can't be the perfect person in your life. It'll never happen, because they aren't God.

You married a flawed individual, but that's not an excuse to abandon your commitment to God and his word. You and I must follow God's commands and walk in the counsel of his word regardless of our spouse's obedience to God.

We all will meet frustrating moments in marriage, yet in those dark moments of life the light must shine brighter. In the end, love always wins. Someone's got to walk in love. That someone should be the one who is a child of Love. So what does this God kind of love look like in action? Let's take advice from Jesus himself.

Luke 6:27–28 (NLT): 27 "But to you who are willing to listen, I say, love your enemies! Do good to those who hate you. 28 Bless those who curse you.

Are you saved to God? Then you're called to love. Another way of saying this would be, rescued from hate to love. We are commanded to love regardless of a person's hateful and mean actions towards us. We love because we are designed to love. As we walk in the power of love it becomes our joy, and not a burden.

Jesus says something that's so powerful in verse 27 "to you who are willing to listen." Even when God himself is giving advice, he gives us the freedom to ignore or obey. He gives us the freedom of choice. That's love without manipulation or coercion. With your God-given freedom, choose acts of love over a grudge.

What's in Your Eye?

Now that you've experienced this grace and mercy from God, you're obligated to show it to your spouse. They need it the most when they've messed up the worst. Most people can show love when everything is going well, but we must strive to show love even when it isn't.

Too often a judgmental attitude dominates in marriage. It's manifested through a constant examination and criticism of their actions. No one wants to be married to a walking faultfinder. They didn't marry you so you could follow their every move and critique their performance. That's a miserable marriage.

Matthew 7:3–5 (NLT): 3 "And why worry about a speck in your friend's eye when you have a log in your own? 4 How can you think of saying to your friend, 'Let me help you get rid of that speck in your eye,' when you can't see past the log in your own eye? 5 Hypocrite! First get rid of the log in your own eye; then you will see well enough to deal with the speck in your friend's eye.

Jesus makes life so simple doesn't he? While we may focus on the splinter in our spouse's eye, Jesus says we need to deal with a log in our own. He could've said before you take the splinter out of their eye remove the splinter out of yours. Instead he clarifies that there's a sin we are irritated by in someone else, but our problems may be greater. It's hypocritical for an imperfect person to highlight the imperfections of others.

Verse 3 uses a unique word to describe our frame of mind when we're caught up in the imperfections of others. He calls it worry when our minds are meditating on their mistakes. Are you so irritated by a person's mistakes that you meditate on them? Maybe that's why he calls our problem a log and theirs a speck. Could it be that while we are meditating on the flaws of others we become bitter, and think that we're better? Now that's a log of a problem.

"Well, you don't understand, I've told them time and again what to do and they continue to get it wrong. They just don't care." My reply to this argument again is, haven't you made commitments to God that you weren't able to fulfill? Aren't you falling short of God's glory, but you sincerely love him?

We all make mistakes, but God doesn't write us off or treat us with an intolerant spirit. He still provides, and holds up his end of the relationship. We must strive to be like our Heavenly Father and offer grace. Grace is undeserved and unearned favor. Meaning your spouse shouldn't have to be good to you before your goodness is extended to them.

"Well, Sean, I'm not God, and I can't just forgive like that." I must say that you're wrong! God's Spirit lives in you and the fruit of the Spirit is love, patience, kindness, meekness, gentleness, longsuffering, and self-control. You've got what it takes to live a godly life towards your spouse if you're willing. Now what may need to happen is that your judgmental perspective must change. Focus on you, and not their imperfections. Determine within yourself that you'll be committed to God no matter what.

Chapter Summary

- You can't force your spouse's readiness level-you can do a few things by faith until they get with the program

- You can pray without ceasing

- You can stay in the place of grace; you'll need faith that God's love will empower you

- Faith it until you make it. You can control your actions and it will eventually impact their reactions

- Regardless of what's happening in your environment, your internal climate must be regulated by God alone

- You married a flawed individual, but that's not an excuse to abandon your commitment to God and His Word.

- Focus on you, not their imperfections

Becoming Intimate Life–Builders

1. Pray for your spouse- Remember that you are one with them and pray with intensity

2. Be gracious to your spouse. Become a conduit of grace and mercy

3. Seek empowerment from God to carry you through

4. Stay true to your commitment to God and His word

5. Focus on what you must do in your marriage and not your spouses inperfections

For Reflection:

- Is your spouse ready to attend the University of Us? If not, what steps will you take to begin faithing it until to make it?

Chapter 22

Come Out of The Closet

Let's face it, sometimes you're in over your head. If you are, then please reach out and get professional counseling. Go to a marriage retreat, or meet with mentors to get the answers you need for healing. Whatever you do, fight for your marriage. If you are embarrassed by your marital struggles, I must tell you, you're not alone. Many couples are facing or have faced what you are going through.

You will remain as sick as your secrets. Whatever sicknesses you try to hide will eventually thrive. Get past your embarrassment and get the help you need. If your car had a flat tire, you'd pull over and place on a spare tire. Almost everyone reading this book should be able to fix that.

But what if the engine had a cracked head gasket? I've had one before and trust me, it's not a quick fix. The majority of us can't fix a major problem like that on our own. This repair needs a specialist to repair it in a special shop with the right replacement parts. I'd look like a fool standing on the side of the road with a cracked head gasket trying to repair what's beyond my ability and immediate resources.

Sometimes in marriage there are problems beyond your personal ability to repair on your own. You need a specialist that can guide you to repair the damage with special parts in a special shop. Just like there's no shame in going to a mechanic, there's no shame in going to a mechanic of marriage to fix broken hearts.

If there's a marriage ministry in a healthy Christian church, go there and get connected. You should also find a healthy couple and ask them to mentor you. You need mentoring from healthy couples. Everyone's advice isn't right for you and your mate.

If at first you don't succeed in a small group or with mentors, try, try again. It's worth it to surround yourself with loving people that will pour wisdom into your life.

Proverbs 27:17 (NLT): As iron sharpens iron, so a friend sharpens a friend.

A dull blade isn't very useful. The purpose of a knife is that it's sharp enough to cut. When we connect with friends and wise people they can sharpen us. Friends, mentors, and counselors sharpen our character. They enable us to become better at marriage and all that God created us to do.

There's nothing wrong with seeking a Christian counselor if you need one. Do your research on whomever you choose to receive counsel from. No matter what you do about wise counsel, please make sure you put yourself in a position to prosper in your marriage.

Even if your marriage is in a healthy place right now, you still need wisdom from great leadership. Solomon gives us great advice in the book of Proverbs:

Proverbs 11:2 (NLT): Pride leads to disgrace, but with humility comes wisdom.

My Prayer for You

Heavenly Father, bless this husband and wife to be a united team. Give them strength for their journey. Unlock dreams and visions within their hearts.

Enable them to work together in harmony to build generational blessings. Allow your joy and peace to manifest within their family as they yield to your Truth. Guide them by the power of your Holy Spirit.

Give this husband and wife wisdom for the ministry of marriage. Grant them multiplied grace and peace towards one another.

I pray that they'll release any pride and walk in humility. I ask you to remind them that they're of one mind, body, and soul. I pray that you enable them to live a life of abundance and blessing.

Father, enable this marriage to show the love of Jesus to their family and to the world. I pray that they'll be intimate life-builders from this day forward.

In Jesus' name, Amen.

Chapter Summary

- Whatever you do, fight for your marriage

- You will remain as sick as your secrets. Get past your embarrassment and get the help you need

- Get connected to a marriage ministry in a healthy Christian church

- You should also find a healthy couple and ask them to mentor you

- There's nothing wrong with seeking a Christian counselor if you need one

Becoming Intimate Life-Builders

1. Pray with and for your spouse daily

2. Get connected to a marriage ministry in a healthy Christian Church

3. Find a healthy couple and ask them to mentor you

4. Seek the help of a Christian counselor if necessary

For Reflection:

- In what areas does your marriage need help, wise counsel or mentoring so that it can become or remain healthy? What friends, mentors or counselors has God led you to sharpen you in your marriage?

Ways to connect with Not Just Roommates!

- Follow us online at: www.notjustroommates.org
- On Twitter: @njroommates
- Like us on Facebook: https://www.facebook.com/njroommates
- On Instagram : @njroommates
- Or search: *crossroadstx* in your app store for Sean Reed's message content

Made in USA - Kendallville, IN
65929_9781537262185
02.01.2024 1408